Management and Treatment of Insanity Acquittees

A Model for the 1990s

Number 41

David Spiegel, M.D.
Series Editor

Management and Treatment of Insanity Acquittees

A Model for the 1990s

By
Joseph D. Bloom, M.D.
Mary H. Williams, M.S., J.D.

American Psychiatric Press, Inc.

Washington, DC
London, England

Note: The authors have worked to ensure that all information in this book concerning drug dosages, schedules, and routes of administration is accurate as of the time of publication and consistent with standards set by the U.S. Food and Drug Administration and the general medical community. As medical research and practice advance, however, therapeutic standards may change. For this reason and because human and mechanical errors sometimes occur, we recommend that readers follow the advice of a physician who is directly involved in their care or in the care of a member of their family.

Books published by the American Psychiatric Press, Inc., represent the views and opinions of the individual authors and do not necessarily represent the policies and opinions of the Press or the American Psychiatric Association.

Manufactured in the United States of America on acid-free paper

First Edition   97   96   95   94   4   3   2   1

American Psychiatric Press, Inc.
1400 K Street, N.W., Washington, DC   20005

Bloom, Joseph D.
    Management and treatment of insanity acquittees : a model for the 1990s / by Joseph D. Bloom, Mary H. Williams.
        p.   cm. — (Progress in psychiatry series : no. 41)
    Includes bibliographical references and index.
    ISBN 0-88048-501-9
    1. Oregon, Psychiatric Security Review Board.   2. Insane, Criminal and dangerous—Oregon.   3. Insane, Criminal and dangerous—Rehabilitation—Oregon.   4. Prisoners—Mental health services—Oregon.   5. Insanity—Jurisprudence—Oregon.   I. Williams, Mary H., M.S.   II. Title.   III. Series: Progress in psychiatry series : 41.
        [DNLM: 1. Mental Disorders—therapy.   2. Insanity Defense.   W1 PR6781L no.41 1994 / WM 100 B655m 1994]
    KFO2966.6.B56   1994
    362.1'08'692—dc20
    DNLM/DLC
    for Library of Congress   93-10876
                                                                                         CIP

British Library Cataloguing in Publication Data
A CIP record is available from the British Library.

This book is dedicated to the memory of Saleem A. Shah, Ph.D. 1931–1992

Contents

Contributors

Douglas A. Bigelow, Ph.D.
Associate Director of Health Economics Planning, Ministry of Health, Province of British Columbia, Victoria, British Columbia, and Adjunct Assistant Professor of Psychiatry, Department of Psychiatry, School of Medicine, Oregon Health Sciences University, Portland, Oregon

Joseph D. Bloom, M.D.
Professor and Chairman, Department of Psychiatry, School of Medicine, Oregon Health Sciences University, Portland, Oregon

Bentson H. McFarland, M.D., Ph.D.
Director, Western Mental Health Research Center, and Associate Professor of Psychiatry, Public Health and Preventive Medicine, School of Medicine, Oregon Health Sciences University, Portland, Oregon; Investigator, Kaiser Permanente Center for Health Research, Portland, Oregon

Jeffrey L. Rogers, J.D.
City Attorney, City of Portland, Oregon; Clinical Professor of Psychiatry, Department of Psychiatry, School of Medicine, Oregon Health Sciences University, Portland, Oregon

Mary H. Williams, M.S., J.D.
Adjunct Assistant Professor of Psychiatry, Department of Psychiatry, School of Medicine, Oregon Health Sciences University, Portland, Oregon

Introduction to the Progress in Psychiatry Series

The Progress in Psychiatry Series is designed to capture in print the excitement that comes from assembling a diverse group of experts from various locations to examine in detail the newest information about a developing aspect of psychiatry. This series emerged as a collaboration between the American Psychiatric Association's (APA) Scientific Program Committee and the American Psychiatric Press, Inc. Great interest is generated by a number of the symposia presented each year at the APA annual meeting, and we realized that much of the information presented there, carefully assembled by people who are deeply immersed in a given area, would unfortunately not appear together in print. The symposia sessions at the annual meetings provide an unusual opportunity for experts who otherwise might not meet on the same platform to share their diverse viewpoints for a period of 3 hours. Some new themes are repeatedly reinforced and gain credence, whereas in other instances disagreements emerge, enabling the audience and now the reader to reach informed decisions about new directions in the field. The Progress in Psychiatry Series allows us to publish and capture some of the best of the symposia and thus provide an in-depth treatment of specific areas that might not otherwise be presented in broader review formats.

Psychiatry is, by nature, an interface discipline, combining the study of mind and brain, of individual and social environments, of the humane and the scientific. Therefore, progress in the field is rarely linear—it often comes from unexpected sources. Furthermore, new developments emerge from an array of viewpoints that do not necessarily provide immediate agreement but rather expert examination of the issues. We intend to present innovative ideas and data that will enable you, the reader, to participate in this process.

We believe the Progress in Psychiatry Series will provide you with an opportunity to review timely, new information in specific fields of interest as they are developing. We hope you find that the excitement of the presentations is captured in the written word and that this book proves to be informative and enjoyable reading.

David Spiegel, M.D.
Series Editor
Progress in Psychiatry Series

Progress in Psychiatry Series Titles

Clinical Advances in Monoamine Oxidase Inhibitor Therapies (#43)
Edited by Sidney H. Kennedy, M.D., F.R.C.P.C.

Catecholamine Function in Posttraumatic Stress Disorder: Emerging Concepts (#42)
Edited by M. Michele Murburg, M.D.

Management and Treatment of Insanity Acquittees: A Model for the 1990s (#41)
Edited by Joseph D. Bloom, M.D., and Mary H. Williams, M.S., J.D.

Chronic Fatigue and Related Immune Deficiency Syndromes (#40)
Edited by Paul J. Goodnick, M.D., and Nancy G. Klimas, M.D.

Psychopharmacology and Psychobiology of Ethnicity (#39)
Edited by Keh-Ming Lin, M.D., M.P.H., Russell E. Poland, Ph.D., and Gayle Nakasaki, M.S.W.

Electroconvulsive Therapy: From Research to Clinical Practice (#38)
Edited by C. Edward Coffey, M.D.

Multiple Sclerosis: A Neuropsychiatric Disorder (#37)
Edited by Uriel Halbreich, M.D.

Biology of Anxiety Disorders (#36)
Edited by Rudolf Hoehn-Saric, M.D., and Daniel R. McLeod, Ph.D.

Psychoimmunology Update (#35)
Edited by Jack M. Gorman, M.D., and Robert M. Kertzner, M.D.

Brain Imaging in Affective Disorders (#34)
Edited by Peter Hauser, M.D.

Positron-Emission Tomography in Schizophrenia Research (#33)
Edited by Nora D. Volkow, M.D., and Alfred P. Wolf, Ph.D.

Mental Retardation: Developing Pharmacotherapies (#32)
Edited by John J. Ratey, M.D.

Current Concepts of Somatization: Research and Clinical Perspectives (#31)
Edited by Laurence J. Kirmayer, M.D., F.R.C.P.C., and James M. Robbins, Ph.D.

Central Nervous System Peptide Mechanisms in Stress and Depression (#30)
Edited by S. Craig Risch, M.D.

Neuropeptides and Psychiatric Disorders (#29)
Edited by Charles B. Nemeroff, M.D., Ph.D.

Negative Schizophrenic Symptoms: Pathophysiology and Clinical Implications (#28)
Edited by John F. Greden, M.D., and Rajiv Tandon, M.D.

The Neuroleptic Nonresponsive Patient: Characterization and Treatment (#27)
Edited by Burt Angrist, M.D., and S. Charles Schulz, M.D.

Combination Pharmacotherapy and Psychotherapy for Depression (#26)
Edited by Donna Manning, M.D., and Allen J. Frances, M.D.

Treatment Strategies for Refractory Depression (#25)
Edited by Steven P. Roose, M.D., and Alexander H. Glassman, M.D.

Biological Rhythms, Mood Disorders, Light Therapy, and the Pineal Gland (#24)
Edited by Mohammad Shafii, M.D., and Sharon Lee Shafii, R.N., B.S.N.

Family Environment and Borderline Personality Disorder (#23)
Edited by Paul Skevington Links, M.D.

Amino Acids in Psychiatric Disease (#22)
Edited by Mary Ann Richardson, Ph.D.

Serotonin in Major Psychiatric Disorders (#21)
Edited by Emil F. Coccaro, M.D., and Dennis L. Murphy, M.D.

Personality Disorders: New Perspectives on Diagnostic Validity (#20)
Edited by John M. Oldham, M.D.

Biological Assessment and Treatment of Posttraumatic Stress Disorder (#19)
Edited by Earl L. Giller, Jr., M.D., Ph.D.

Depression in Schizophrenia (#18)
Edited by Lynn E. DeLisi, M.D.

Depression and Families: Impact and Treatment (#17)
Edited by Gabor I. Keitner, M.D.

Depressive Disorders and Immunity (#16)
Edited by Andrew H. Miller, M.D.

Treatment of Tricyclic-Resistant Depression (#15)
Edited by Irl L. Extein, M.D.

Current Approaches to the Prediction of Violence (#14)
Edited by David A. Brizer, M.D., and Martha L. Crowner, M.D.

Tardive Dyskinesia: Biological Mechanisms and Clinical Aspects (#13)
Edited by Marion E. Wolf, M.D., and Aron D. Mosnaim, Ph.D.

Eating Behavior in Eating Disorders (#12)
Edited by B. Timothy Walsh, M.D.

Cerebral Hemisphere Function in Depression (#11)
Edited by Marcel Kinsbourne, M.D.

Psychobiology of Bulimia (#10)
Edited by James I. Hudson, M.D., and Harrison G. Pope, Jr., M.D.

Psychiatric Pharmacosciences of Children and Adolescents (#9)
Edited by Charles Popper, M.D.

Biopsychosocial Aspects of Bereavement (#8)
Edited by Sidney Zisook, M.D.

Medical Mimics of Psychiatric Disorders (#7)
Edited by Irl Extein, M.D., and Mark S. Gold, M.D.

Can Schizophrenia Be Localized in the Brain? (#6)
Edited by Nancy C. Andreasen, M.D., Ph.D.

The Psychiatric Implications of Menstruation (#5)
Edited by Judith H. Gold, M.D., F.R.C.P.C.

Post-Traumatic Stress Disorder in Children (#4)
Edited by Spencer Eth, M.D., and Robert S. Pynoos, M.D., M.P.H.

Treatment of Affective Disorders in the Elderly (#3)
Edited by Charles A. Shamoian, M.D.

Premenstrual Syndrome: Current Findings and Future Directions (#2)
Edited by Howard J. Osofsky, M.D., Ph.D., and
Susan J. Blumenthal, M.D.

The Borderline: Current Empirical Research (#1)
Edited by Thomas H. McGlashan, M.D.

Preface

This book was written with several purposes in mind. First, it is a program report, exploring a system designed for the management and treatment of Oregon's insanity acquittees. The program has national implications. The Psychiatric Security Review Board (PSRB), which is the cornerstone of the program, was described in 1983 by the American Psychiatric Association as a potential national model (1) for the management of insanity acquittees. Connecticut (2) and Utah have set up review board models and a number of states have explored the possibility of setting up such programs. This book can be of assistance to individuals working in other jurisdictions as they decide on the model that is best for their situation.

We hope that this book will also further the development of a mental health services research agenda for forensic populations. There is a critical need for research in this area, because of the unfortunate reality that our nation's jails and prisons now house many seriously mentally ill individuals. We expect that mental health treatment resources will continue to erode, and mentally ill individuals will continue to enter the criminal justice system. For these reasons, a services research agenda focused on this system needs to be encouraged in the 1990s (3–5).

There is little doubt that statutes and case law have profound effects on mental health services. Laws direct who is to be served and in what order of priority. A change in a law—whether generated by a legislature or by the judiciary—can, in short order, dramatically alter the delivery of mental health services and can also, for better or worse, significantly affect the lives of seriously mentally ill people (6). Witness the major changes (some positive and many negative) that are apparent in the lives of mentally ill people and were brought about by the wholesale deinstitutionalization of mentally ill patients from psychiatric hospitals (7, 8).

Over the years, we have filled many requests to provide information about the PSRB to members of the National Alliance for the Mentally Ill (NAMI) from across this country. Members of this organization have had the most interest in this program because it is their relatives who are the insanity acquittees, and it is their relatives who are in the jails and prisons. We hope that the material in this book will prove helpful to members of NAMI and, of course, to others who struggle on a daily basis with the problems of severely mentally ill people and the inadequacies of the service system.

This book represents the work of many people who have contributed to this research effort for well over a decade. We use the pronoun "we" often in the book. We refer here primarily to the two principal authors and to a group of major collaborators who have worked with us over the years, including Jeffrey L. Rogers, J.D., Douglas A. Bigelow, Ph.D., Spero Manson, Ph.D., and Scott Reichlin, M.D. We owe much to these people. Their ideas and work are part of this book. In addition we have received substantial assistance from Bentson H. McFarland, M.D., Ph.D., and Greg Clarke, Ph.D., from the Western Mental Health Research Center. Both the PSRB and the Oregon Mental Health and Developmental Disabilities Services Division have been very supportive of our research efforts over the years. In particular, Kathleen Haley, J.D., Richard Lippincott, M.D., Barry Kast, M.S.W., J. Donald Bray, M.D., James H. Shore, M.D., Jo Mahler, M.S., and Nancy Hashimoto have been extremely helpful. We received external financial support for this project from the National Institute of Mental Health from grants MH-42221 and MH-43458. Finally, on the national level, we wish to thank Loren H. Roth, M.D., for his long-term commitment to this research project.

REFERENCES

1. Insanity Defense Work Group: American Psychiatric Association statement on the insanity defense. Am J Psychiatry 140:681–688, 1983
2. Scott D, Zonana H, Gatz M: Monitoring insanity acquitees: Connecticut's Psychiatric Security Review Board. Hosp Community Psychiatry 41:980–984, 1990

3. National Institute of Mental Health: The Future of Mental Health Services Research (DHHS Publ No ADM-89-1600). Edited by Taube CA, Mechanic D, Hohmann AA. Washington, DC, U.S. Government Printing Office, 1989

4. National Institute of Mental Health: Caring for People With Severe Mental Disorders: A National Plan of Research to Improve Services (DHHS Publ No ADM-91-1762). Washington, DC, U.S. Government Printing Office, 1991

5. Steadman HJ, Braff J: Defendants not guilty by reason of insanity, in Mentally Disordered Offenders: Perspectives From Law and Social Science. Edited by Monahan J, Steadman HJ. New York, Plenum, 1983, pp 109–129

6. Bloom JD, Faulkner LR, Shore JH, et al: The young adult chronic patient and the legal system: a system's analysis. New Dir Ment Health Serv 19:37–50, 1983

7. Miller RD: Involuntary Civil Commitment of the Mentally Ill in the Post-Reform Era. Springfield, IL, Charles C Thomas, 1987

8. Isaac RJ, Armat VC: Madness in the Streets—How Psychiatry and the Law Abandoned the Mentally Ill. New York, Free Press, 1990

Chapter 1

The Oregon Psychiatric Security Review Board in a National Perspective

INTRODUCTION

The insanity defense represents an attempt to accommodate the requirement for criminal responsibility in the criminal law with the presence of serious mental illness. As such, it represents an important conceptual underpinning of the criminal law. The criminal law is built on the presumption of rational action on the part of the offender who chooses to commit an illegal act. Over the centuries, Anglo-American law has been confronted with a relatively small number of defendants who have such serious mental disorders that the application to them of a rational model of conduct appears absurd (1). As a result, most jurisdictions have an insanity defense.

The insanity defense continues its existence today mainly because there appears to be no generally accepted and satisfactory way around it (2, 3). From a utilitarian point of view, it is designed to weed out from the criminal justice process a small number of the most seriously mentally ill offenders and to leave the remaining defendants to the sanctions of the criminal law. Those removed from the criminal justice system by a successful insanity defense most often have alternative sanctions applied to them. The system described in this book is one example of such a sanction. It requires that those individuals who have successfully raised an insanity defense in Oregon courts, and who receive what we have called an "insanity sentence" (4, 5), be served within the mental health system. In this chapter, we describe the Oregon system by focusing on the roles of the trial court, the Psychiatric Security Review Board (the PSRB, or the Board), and

1

the Oregon Mental Health and Developmental Disabilities Services Division (the Division) in relation to insanity acquittees.

HOW THE OREGON SYSTEM WORKS

The legal process that leads to the insanity verdict in Oregon is similar to other jurisdictions. In 1971 the legislature adopted the American Law Institute test based on the Model Penal Code (6). In designing the PSRB in 1977, the Oregon legislature left the American Law Institute language of the insanity defense intact and did not attempt, at that time, to alter the process that led to the insanity verdict. Instead, the legislature created a management system wherein the PSRB assumed the responsibility for insanity acquittees at the end of the trial phase of the criminal justice process.

Oregon's 1977 reforms resulted from public and professional concerns about the management of insanity acquittees committed to the state's forensic hospital. The system in existence in the 1970s in Oregon was fairly typical of what exists in many, if not most, jurisdictions in this country today, in which the trial court judge and the forensic hospital control the disposition of an individual following a successful insanity verdict. In the move toward reform, there were concerns that there were too many decisionmakers in the process with potentially more than 140 circuit and district court judges in the state. There were concerns about great variation in the quality of decisions made by this large number of judges. There were concerns about aspects of the functioning of the forensic hospital, and a fear that patients were prematurely being recommended for release, with the result that the public safety was threatened. There were concerns about lack of continuity of care in relation to community follow-up of released patients. There were the inevitable and sometimes dramatic cases that came to public attention and that illustrated the flaws in the system and focused blame on the hospital, the courts, and the patients.

The 1977 Legislative Assembly created the PSRB and defined the relationship between the PSRB and the trial court. The legislature did not define the role of the Division in this process. However, since 1978, a delineation of responsibilities between the Board and the Division has evolved. What follows is a description of these roles and responsibilities for the trial court, the Board, and the Division.

The Role of the Trial Court

The insanity defense focuses on the individual's mental state at the time of the alleged criminal act. Once an insanity verdict has been rendered, the trial court judge conducts a form of sentencing hearing to determine the disposition of the case. At this hearing, the judge in Oregon has several choices. If the judge finds that the insanity acquittee is no longer mentally ill and/or no longer dangerous to the public, the judge must then release that person with no further supervision. We estimate that very few insanity acquittees are released under this provision. Typically, the judge finds that the insanity acquittee still has a mental illness and continues to present some danger to the public. Upon making such a finding, the judge must then place the insanity acquittee under the jurisdiction of the PSRB.

The trial court must also fix the maximum length of PSRB jurisdiction by determining the specific crime of which the individual would have been found guilty had there not been an insanity verdict. The maximum sentence for that crime sets the length of the Board's jurisdiction within the range of 1 year for a misdemeanor, to lifetime jurisdiction for murder. This is a very important provision, because it sets a durational limit to the length of time that an individual insanity acquittee can remain under the jurisdiction of the Board. These acquittees cannot be confined for indeterminate periods.

We have called this time period the "insanity sentence," and we will use this term throughout this book to refer to the maximum length of the Board's jurisdiction over an individual insanity acquittee. It is analogous to a criminal sentence, with a fixed length of maximum jurisdiction determined by the particular crime. Like a criminal sentence, there frequently is an institutional component (hospitalization) and a community component (conditional release with supervision).

Under Oregon's PSRB system, the trial court judge also determines whether an identified victim wants notification of all Board hearings involving the particular acquittee. Finally, the judge determines whether the insanity acquittee initially will be placed in the forensic hospital or in the community on conditional release. At this point, all involvement with the trial court ends and the responsibility for the future management of these insanity acquittees is transferred to the PSRB.

The Psychiatric Security Review Board

As we mentioned previously, the Oregon legislature created the PSRB in 1977 and transferred the legal responsibility for insanity acquittees from the trial courts to the jurisdiction of this new entity (7). The legislature mandated that protection of the general public was to be the main concern of the PSRB. This is clearly articulated in statute:

> In determining whether a person should be committed to a state hospital, conditionally released or discharged, the Board shall have as its primary concern the protection of society (8).

This legislative mandate was later supported by the Oregon Supreme Court in a widely reported case, *Cain v. Rijken* (9).

Structure of the Board

We have described the PSRB in some detail in past publications (10, 11); however, it is important for the reader's understanding of the material presented in this book that we summarize the key elements of the system. The PSRB is a state agency administratively located within the Executive Department and administered by an executive director. Since its inception, there have been four executive directors, all attorneys. The Board itself comprises five part-time Board members, each appointed by the Governor for 4-year terms. By statute, the Board comprises an attorney with experience in criminal justice practice, a psychiatrist, a psychologist, an individual with a background in corrections, and a lay citizen.

Hearings

The Board conducts approximately 300 full hearings each year. As a consequence of these hearings, either no change is made in placement, or the individual may be conditionally released into the community, returned to the hospital on a revocation of conditional release, or discharged from the Board's jurisdiction. At any of these hearings, the Board may order modifications made in current treatment plans.

Hearings regarding individual insanity acquittees take place on a weekly basis involving panels of three Board members. When the three members of the panel are unable to reach a unanimous decision, the matter is considered by the full Board.

Hearings differ in terms of how they are initiated, what action is requested, what burden of proof the Board must consider in evaluating information, and what ultimate determination the Board makes regarding the requested action. There are a number of ways by which an individual may come to the Board for a hearing.

Mandatory hearings. The statutes mandate a hearing within 90 days for individuals initially hospitalized after assignment to the PSRB. The statutes also require a review for those individuals who have been hospitalized for a 2-year period when no other hearing has been held within this time period.

Mental health staff requested hearings. The hospital staff or community mental health staff monitoring conditional release may request a hearing at any time for Board consideration of conditional release, revocation, and/or discretionary discharge.

Acquittee initiated hearings. Insanity acquittees may request a Board hearing, not more frequently than once every 6 months. These hearings may include requests for conditional release, modification of the conditional release plans, or discharge.

Revocation hearings. After an order of revocation for violation of conditional release, the Board is required to hold a hearing
within 20 days.

Status review hearings. At any time the Board may, on its
own motion, call for a status review to discuss an acquittee. The
status review is held to determine whether modification of a
Board order is appropriate.

When the insanity acquittee requests a hearing before the
Board to consider a conditional release or a discharge, the individual bears the burden of establishing by a preponderance of the
evidence that a change in placement is warranted. In all other
cases—mandatory review hearings and those requested by the
treatment team—the state bears the burden of presenting evidence to support the placement recommendations.

General Powers of the PSRB

Once the trial court judge completes his or her required activities,
the PSRB assumes responsibility for the insanity acquittee for the
duration of the insanity sentence. The Board governs the movement of acquittees between the hospital and the community. The
Board may conditionally release hospitalized acquittees to a community treatment program, or the Board may order a revocation
of conditional release and return the person to the forensic hospital. If at any point during the insanity sentence the Board determines that an individual under its jurisdiction is no longer
mentally ill or no longer dangerous, then by statute the Board
must release the person from its jurisdiction.

Conditional Release

As we will discuss at several points in this book, the development
of well-supervised conditional release for insanity acquittees is
one of the key innovations of the Oregon system. The framework
for conditional release is set out in statute as follows:

If the Board determines that the person presents a substantial
danger to others but can be adequately controlled with supervi-

sion and treatment if conditionally released and that necessary supervision and treatment are available, the Board may order the person conditionally released, subject to those supervisory orders of the Board as are in the best interests of justice, the protection of society and the welfare of the person. (12)

This statute sets out the legislative priorities in two important areas. First, the individual must not only be ready for conditional release, but supervision and treatment must also be available. Second, the legislative priorities clearly establish that protection of the public takes precedence over the treatment and welfare of the insanity acquittee.

Conditional release is governed by a conditional release order developed by the Board in conjunction with the forensic hospital staff and the community treatment program that will monitor the conditional release. The order sets out both the general and special conditions that represent the agreement between the Board, the community mental health treatment program, and the insanity acquittee regarding the conditional release.

As illustrated by a 1986 order, the following areas are covered in a typical conditional release order.

Housing. The individual must live in a specific group home and is prohibited from changing residence without the notification and approval of his case manager. The staff of the group home must observe the individual taking his medications.

Mental health aftercare. The conditionally released person must participate in a treatment program coordinated by the staff of a specific community mental health program. He also must submit to drug screens at the request of the staff of the county mental health program. Program staff must monitor the medications received by the subject.

Reporting responsibilities. The order names a case manager from the county mental health program designated with the primary responsibility for the case. This case manager agrees to report to the Board on a monthly basis (or more often when indicated) regarding the individual's condition and compliance with the program. In addition, the case manager agrees to notify the Board, at any time, if the individual violates the conditional release plan.

Other requirements. This order prohibits the conditionally released person from drinking any beverages containing alcohol and prohibits him from driving a motor vehicle. Another special condition prohibits family visits without advance approval from the case manager.

The provisions included in this order are analogous to those reported from New York (13), which include conditions of release related to treatment, housing, medication, restriction on the use of alcohol and drugs, restriction of contact with the victim, and reports on a regular basis to a district attorney. The main difference is that reports in Oregon go to the Board, whereas in New York reports are submitted to a district attorney.

Revocation

The ability to revoke a conditional release is an extremely important feature of this system. This is set out in statute as follows:

> If at any time while the person is under the jurisdiction of the Board it appears to the Board or its chairman that the person has violated the terms of the conditional release or that the mental health of the individual has changed, the Board or its chairman may order the person returned to a state hospital designated by the Mental Health and Developmental Disabilities Services Division for evaluation and treatment. (14)

This statute makes it very clear that conditional release can be revoked when the conditionally released person either has violated the terms of the conditional release agreement or is experiencing a deterioration of his or her mental status.

In the New York system described previously, an order of revocation can only be obtained after a court hearing, where the subject's current dangerousness is demonstrated. This requirement results in a much lower rate of revocation in New York State when compared with Oregon or with Maryland (see Chapter 4).

Discharge From PSRB Jurisdiction

The PSRB also makes decisions regarding the question of discharge of an acquittee from its jurisdiction. Discharge occurs when the insanity sentence is completed or when the Board determines, at one of its regular hearings, that an individual is no longer mentally ill and/or no longer dangerous. We have chosen to call this latter form of discharge a "discretionary discharge," because the Board has discretion in making these findings. However, the Board is compelled by statute to discharge an insanity acquittee if they find, by a preponderance of the evidence, that the individual is "no longer affected by mental disease or defect, or if so affected, no longer presents a substantial danger to others which requires regular medical care, medication, supervision or treatment" (15).

There is another statutory section that is critical in relation to the functioning of the Board and the question of discharge:

> For purposes of this section, a person affected by a mental disease or defect in a state of remission is considered to have a mental disease or defect. A person whose mental disease or defect may, with reasonable medical probability, occasionally become active and when it becomes active will render the person a danger to others, shall not be discharged. The person shall continue under such supervision and treatment as the Board deems necessary to protect the person and others. (16)

This section, in essence, defines chronic mental illnesses, such as schizophrenia or bipolar disorder, and makes it clear that acquittees with these illnesses, even if they are in remission, may be retained under Board jurisdiction. This particular feature of the PSRB statute also lessens the debate that plagues many jurisdictions about the prediction of dangerousness (17, 18) and, in part, transfers the debate to a discussion of the natural history of chronic mental illness and its care and management.

This statutory section also distinguishes an insanity acquittee in Oregon from an individual committed to a state hospital under the Oregon civil commitment statutes. The civil commitment statutes focus on the person's current illness coupled with dangerousness and/or grave disability, and release is mandatory if an individual currently does not meet criteria. Once discharged from the jurisdiction of the Board, neither the trial court nor the Board has any continuing authority over the released individual. At the end of the insanity sentence, the state has the option of instituting civil commitment procedures to retain custody of the individual if it is believed that the individual meets civil commitment criteria. Once civilly committed in Oregon (19), an individual may be hospitalized for up to 180 days. At the end of this time period, the person must either be released or be subject to a recommitment hearing.

The Mental Health and Developmental Disabilities Services Division

The Division has a critical role in the Oregon system. Whereas the PSRB is primarily responsible for placement of insanity acquittees either in the hospital or on conditional release in the community, the Division is responsible for the treatment provided to these individuals whether in the hospital or in the community.

The Role of the Forensic Hospital

Hospital care is organized in a fairly typical fashion at the Oregon State Hospital forensic unit, which is located in Salem, Oregon. While the individual is hospitalized, the treatment plan is the responsibility of the hospital staff. However, major alterations in the plan, such as off-campus passes, must have prior approval of the Board. Interestingly, treatment refusal is not adjudicated before the Board. Instead, it is handled by administrative rule promulgated by the Division to handle treatment refusal of civilly committed patients, of those individuals found incompetent to stand trial, and of insanity acquittees (20–22).

The Role of the Community Mental Health System

The community care system is a unique feature of the PSRB model. The legislature provided funds to the Division for the community care of insanity acquittees and placed these funds in the Division's budget, not in the budget of the PSRB. The Division disperses these funds to community treatment programs for care of conditionally released insanity acquittees.

Community mental health treatment services in Oregon are provided on a contractual basis between the Division and community mental health programs, most of which are part of county government. Initially, many of the community programs were quite reluctant to accept PSRB clients. However, in the early years of the PSRB, there were a few programs willing to treat conditionally released insanity acquittees. These programs demonstrated that it was possible to successfully manage these acquittees in the community. Currently, there is general acceptance of the conditionally released acquittee throughout the community mental health system.

The community system evolved for several reasons. First, community programs got involved in the treatment of conditionally released insanity acquittees on a voluntary basis. Second, programs willing to treat these individuals received separate payments for these clients. Programs were not asked to displace voluntary patients in order to serve involuntary insanity acquittees. Third, major changes took place in the Oregon mental health system around the same time that the PSRB was created. These key features eventually allowed the PSRB and the Division to develop a mutually supportive and coherent program.

The evolution of Oregon's community mental health program mirrored many of the important changes that took place nationally (23, 24) in the late 1970s and early 1980s. Major reforms took place in the community mental health center program in the late 1970s (25), with a refocus of the program on the problems of chronically mentally ill people as illustrated by such major initiatives as the community support program (26, 27).

In 1977, the National Institute of Mental Health awarded a 4-year grant to the Division to begin to develop community support programs for chronically mentally ill people. In 1979, the Legislative Assembly codified the focus on this population with the passage of a statute aimed at improving the quality of life for chronically mentally ill patients by developing community support and residential services for these patients (28). Among other provisions, the law directed the Division to prepare written plans and case management services for each chronically mentally ill person discharged from a state hospital. The legislature further directed the Division to use discretionary funds to implement the discharge plan, including the use of funds for transportation, medication, recreation, socialization, day treatment, and work activity services for chronically mentally ill people.

This legislation prepared the way for major changes in the organization of the state mental health system. By legislative action, in 1981, the state recognized chronically mentally ill people as the major priority population to be served by the public mental health system. The state reorganized the community mental health program into a series of discrete service elements. The centerpiece of the reorganized system was the community support service element, which included the provision of case management services, medication monitoring, day treatment, and socialization programs. Other service elements included residential services, precommitment services, less intensive outpatient counseling, and medication monitoring services. With this reorganization, the Division created a separate service element for PSRB community services. The Division developed this service element along the lines of a community support program for conditionally released insanity acquittees.

From our preliminary research, and anticipating data that will be presented in this book, this reorganization focusing on problems of chronically mentally ill people was extremely fortuitous. As we shall demonstrate, insanity acquittees in the Oregon system represent a subgroup of the chronically mentally ill population. This focus on chronically mentally ill people developed a commonality of interests between the Board and the Division. States that have not adopted this focus will encounter great difficulties in implementing an outpatient program for chronically mentally ill offenders. It will be difficult to get their outpatient therapists to deal with this patient population. This difficulty will be further complicated by requiring these mental health professionals to deal with a subset of chronically mentally ill patients who also have involvement in the criminal justice system. It also will be difficult for therapists to alter their traditional roles and function like case managers, who are required to report to a regulatory body like the Board or a court on a regular basis.

Liability Concerns of Community
Mental Health Programs

Another significant problem in the development of community care for insanity acquittees relates to concerns on the part of community mental health administrators and professionals about liability issues. There is general feeling among these professionals that they will be subject to an increased risk of malpractice actions stemming from their involvement with conditionally released insanity acquittees, a population defined by statute as dangerous. These general concerns became acute in Oregon following two civil suits brought against community programs. (We describe crimes charged against conditionally released insanity acquittees in Chapter 4.) These civil suits resulted from the two most serious criminal acts committed by conditionally released insanity acquittees. One suit resulted from the involvement of an insanity acquittee in the vehicular death of two individuals (see *Cain v. Rijken*) and the other resulted from an incident in which an insanity acquittee killed his mother. This 1985 case crystallized fears among community mental health providers regarding liability (29) and resulted in the Division's adopting a plan to provide liability coverage for programs treating insanity acquittees in the community.

There are important public policy reasons for the PSRB, the Division, and the legislature to extend liability protection to community mental health programs. Such protection fosters the overall goals of the program and has a cost-saving dimension (30). Although there is general fear of the forensic mental patient, community treatment facilities are critical to the successful operation of programs similar to the one described in this book. Liability protection became another important prong in the development of this cooperative program.

CONCLUSION

This chapter described the development of the PSRB as a separate agency in state government designed to manage Oregon's insanity acquittees. There are several important features that make a Review Board model attractive compared with a traditional management system, which is dependent on trial court judges as the arbitrators of hospitalization and release of insanity acquittees. These advantages include the centralization of authority in a five-member Board, which provides the opportunity for more consistent application of rules and resources by a Board that has developed specialized knowledge of the patient population and of the resources available to care for them.

Most important for this chapter, however, are the features of the Oregon statutory scheme that relate to the question of coercion and fairness. Several areas will be mentioned and discussed in detail in later chapters.

First is the durational limit on the insanity sentence. This is extremely important. In other jurisdictions in the United States, it is possible for insanity acquittees to be confined in security hospitals for an indeterminate period of time, as long as they remain mentally ill and are determined to be dangerous. Given the difficulties in predicting which mentally ill people will in fact be dangerous, this type of indeterminate commitment can lead to an unfair burden being placed on insanity acquittees. A similar burden is not placed even on recidivist criminal offenders, who must be released after their penal sentence expires.

A second critical feature of the Oregon system is the availability of conditional release for insanity acquittees, monitored community treatment, and the availability of prompt revocation.

A third important area relates to the role of the mental health authority in the overall system developed for insanity acquittees. The refocus of the mental health system on chronically mentally ill people was a key development in this program, as was the realization that many of Oregon's insanity acquittees are chronically mentally ill individuals who could be treated in outpatient programs based on community support models. Community-based treatment satisfies modern treatment principles, which emphasize the integration of chronically mentally ill people back into community life. Jurisdictions whose mental health programs have not made this transition in focus will encounter great difficulties in implementing outpatient programs for chronically mentally ill offenders.

The remainder of this book describes this system using data derived from a long-term research project designed to further characterize Oregon's insanity acquittees and to empirically investigate aspects of the system designed to care for them.

REFERENCES

1. Rex v Arnold, 16 How. St. Tr. 695, (1724) at 764
2. Keilitz I, Fulton JP: The Insanity Defense and its Alternates. Williamsburg, VA, National Center for State Courts, 1984
3. Low PW, Jeffries JC, Bonnie RJ: The Trial of John W. Hinckley, Jr.: A Case Study in the Insanity Defense. Mineola, NY, Foundation Press, 1986
4. Rogers JL, Bloom JD, Manson SM: State's insanity defense: an alternative form of sentence. Oregon State Bar Bulletin July 1982, pp 4–6
5. Rogers JL, Bloom JD: The insanity sentence: Oregon's Psychiatric Security Review Board. Behavioral Sciences and the Law 3:69–84, 1985
6. Model Penal Code, 4.01 (2) (Tent. Draft No. 4) (1955)
7. Oregon Revised Statutes §161.319–161.351, §161.385–161.395, 1977
8. Oregon Revised Statutes §161.336(10)
9. Cain v Rijken, 74 Or. App. 76, 700 P.2d 1061 (1985); Cain v Rijken, 300 Or. 706, 717 P.2d 140 (1986)
10. Rogers JL, Bloom JD, Manson SM: Oregon's reform of the insanity defense system. Hosp Community Psychiatry 33:1022–1023, 1982
11. Rogers JL, Bloom JD, Manson SM: Oregon's Psychiatric Security Review Board: a comprehensive system for managing insanity acquittees, in Mental Health and Law: Research and Policy. Annals of the American Academy of Political and Social Sciences 484:86–99, 1986
12. Oregon Revised Statutes §161.336 (1)
13. McGreevy MA, Steadman HJ, Dvoskin JA, et al: New York State's system of managing insanity acquittees in the community. Hosp Community Psychiatry 42:512–517, 1991
14. Oregon Revised Statutes §161.336 (5)
15. Oregon Revised Statutes §161.351 (1)
16. Oregon Revised Statutes §161.351 (2)
17. Bloom JD, Rogers JL: The legal basis of forensic psychiatry: statutorily mandated psychiatric diagnoses. Am J Psychiatry 144:847–853, 1987

18. Monahan J: The Clinical Prediction of Violent Behavior (DHHS Publ No ADM-81-921). Rockville, MD, National Institute of Mental Health, 1981
19. Oregon Revised Statutes §§426.005–426.390
20. Godard SL, Bloom JD, Williams MH, et al: The right to refuse treatment in Oregon: a two-year statewide experience. Behavioral Sciences and the Law 4:293–304, 1986
21. Young JT, Bloom JD, Faulkner LR, et al: Treatment refusal among forensic inpatients. Bull Am Acad Psychiatry Law 15:5–15, 1987
22. Williams MH, Bloom JD, Faulkner LR, et al: Treatment refusal and length of hospitalization of insanity acquittees. Bull Am Acad Psychiatry Law 16:279–285, 1988
23. Bloom JD, Cutler DL, Faulkner LR, et al: The evolution of Oregon's public psychiatry training program. New Dir Ment Health Serv 44:113–121, 1989
24. Foley HA, Sharfstein SS: Madness and Government: Who Cares for the Mentally Ill? Washington, DC, American Psychiatric Press, 1983
25. President's Commission on Mental Health: Report to the President, Vol 1. Washington, DC, U.S. Government Printing Office, 1978
26. National Institute of Mental Health: A Network for Caring—The Community Support Program of the National Institute of Mental Health (DHHS Publ No ADM-81-1063). Washington, DC, U.S. Government Printing Office, 1982
27. Stein LI (ed): Community Support Systems for the Long-Term Patient (New Directions for Mental Health Services, Vol 2). San Francisco, CA, Jossey-Bass, 1979
28. Oregon Revised Statutes §§426.490—426.500
29. Bloom JD: Limiting liability for mandated outpatient treatment of dangerous outpatients. International Journal of Offender Therapy and Comparative Criminology 32:5–8, 1988
30. Bigelow DA, Bloom JD, Williams MH: Costs of managing insanity acquittees under a Psychiatric Security Review Board system. Hosp Community Psychiatry 41:613–621, 1990

Chapter 2

The Psychiatric Security Review Board in a Legal Context

Jeffrey L. Rogers, J.D.

U ntil 1977, Oregon followed a well-marked path in its handling of the insanity defense, utilizing typical criteria for
determining legal insanity and employing typical mechanisms
following insanity verdicts. In 1977, the state legislature made
dramatic changes in the postverdict system, without changing
the insanity defense itself.

For many decades, the state used a modified M'Naughton
insanity test: the defendant had the burden of proving that he or
she was unable to distinguish right from wrong as a result of
mental disease or defect. In the early 1970s, the Oregon legislature
adopted the American Law Institute's (ALI) Model Penal Code
test: a defendant is not responsible if, as a result of mental disease
or defect, he or she lacked substantial capacity either to appreci-
ate the criminality of his or her conduct or to conform his or her
conduct to the requirements of the law. With a few modifications
discussed in this chapter, the ALI test is still used in Oregon.

Before 1977, Oregon also handled disposition of insanity
acquittees in a typical fashion. The trial court could commit the
defendant to a state hospital while retaining jurisdiction over the
defendant. Alternatively, the court could allow the defendant to

Portions of this chapter are reprinted with permission from "1981 Oregon Legislation Relating to the Insanity Defense and the Psychiatric Security Review
Board," *Willamette Law Review,* Volume 18, Number 1, 23–48, Winter 1982.

remain in the community and supervise the defendant in a manner similar to probation. Finally, the court could release the defendant from court jurisdiction. In each case, the court was the final decisionmaker.

In 1977, the Oregon Legislative Assembly undertook an experiment unique in the United States. The legislature left the insanity test intact but made radical changes in the handling of insanity acquittees by creating the Psychiatric Security Review Board (PSRB). Many expected that the innovative PSRB would be the target of multiple, and perhaps fatal, legal challenges. However, 16 years later, the system is firmly established and widely supported, having survived a relatively low level of judicial testing and legislative debate.

This chapter examines the legal basis of the PSRB and highlights some of the salient case law and statutory amendments during PSRB's first decade and a half.

DEVELOPMENT OF THE PSRB

Problems Inherent Under the Old System

As noted, prior to 1977, individual judges maintained jurisdiction over defendants in their courtrooms who were found not guilty by reason of insanity. This statutory scheme required judges to determine if such individuals should be committed to a state psychiatric hospital. If a judge committed an individual, the judge then had the responsibility for deciding when to release that person into the community. In practice, this meant that when the hospital staff thought the individual was ready for conditional release or discharge, the staff would petition the judge and travel with the patient to the court for a hearing. Unfortunately, judges had only limited opportunities to monitor a person's progress in the hospital and often could only defer completely to the recommendations of the hospital staff concerning the patient's release. Although the recommendations were well motivated, they understandably reflected a clinical rather than a legal or public safety perspective. Furthermore, without the necessary funds or personnel, judges were unable to create effective conditional release programs, to monitor the performance of individuals on conditional release, or to return individuals to the hospital if their mental health deteriorated, rendering them dangerous. Thus, judges released many insanity acquittees into the community prematurely, without adequate treatment or safeguards.

At the same time, the Oregon Mental Health and Developmental Disabilities Division (the Division) was concerned with an increasing number of insanity acquittees and the overcrowded forensic wards of the state hospital (1). This situation increased the pressure to release patients from the hospitals after a very short stay. Several experts, as well as the public, perceived that early release defendants frequently committed new crimes, potentially escaping responsibility once again by claiming insanity (2).

Creation of the PSRB

The Governor's Task Force on Corrections and a Division task force studied the insanity defense problem and issued a 1976 report concluding that the system was not working well (3). The PSRB, created to be independent of both the Division and the judiciary, was an attempt to bring order to this perceived chaos.

Effective January 1, 1978, the Board automatically assumed responsibility for all persons found not guilty by reason of insanity and for all persons still under court supervision who previously had been found not guilty by reason of insanity. However, in many instances, the courts had lost track of those under their jurisdiction, which provided a graphic illustration of a major problem of the old system. The courts eventually located 152 such individuals and transferred their supervision to the Board.

EARLY EVOLUTION OF THE BOARD

The Experimental Period: 1978–1980

The 1977 legislature included a sunset provision in the Board's enabling legislation because of uncertainty about whether the

Board would be effective (4). The Board would terminate July 1, 1981, unless the legislature renewed it.

Because the Oregon Legislative Assembly meets biennially, there would be only one chance to refine the statutory scheme before the Board was scheduled to sunset. However, the 1979 legislature made only minor changes to the statutes—clarifying responsibility for paying lawyers appointed to represent indigent defendants appearing before the Board, reallocating the respective responsibilities of the trial court and the PSRB for the initial decisions about an insanity acquittee, and clarifying that revocation orders of the Board gave authority to police to take the defendant into custody for a hearing before the PSRB. This lack of extensive amendments reflected general acceptance of the new system and foreshadowed the results of the thorough legislative review that was undertaken in 1981.

Meanwhile, the first cases involving the PSRB system were making their way into the Oregon appellate courts. Not surprisingly, the first case included a claim that the statutory provisions for supervision by the PSRB violated the constitutional rights to due process and equal protection (5). But the court never reached the constitutional issues. Instead, the Oregon Court of Appeals dismissed the claim, ruling that the statutes did not provide for an appeal from the order of the trial court placing the defendant under the PSRB. Rather, the defendant should have waited and appealed the order of the PSRB at its first hearing on the defendant.

The legislature later amended the statutes to provide a right of appeal from the trial court's order. But the decision of the court of appeals had set the tone: the PSRB system would remain remarkably immune to constitutional challenges, even though the legislature gave the Board highly intrusive powers over defendants and the authority to exercise those powers, including summary revocation of conditional release, with relatively few procedural protections for defendants.

In December 1978, the court of appeals issued its first ruling in a case challenging a PSRB order (6). The Board had revoked a defendant's conditional release after police received an anonymous phone tip that the defendant had threatened suicide. The revocation order demonstrated how summarily the Board was willing to act to fulfill its statutory mission of protecting public safety. The court of appeals reversed the Board's order, holding that there was insufficient evidence to show that the defendant presented a substantial danger to himself, which in the first years of the PSRB was one basis for PSRB supervision and revocation of release. But, once again, the court turned its ruling into a merely technical victory for the defendant. The court rejected the defendant's claim that he should have been discharged from PSRB jurisdiction, noting that he had not specifically applied for discharge.

The small number of appellate decisions during the next year and a half likewise provided no relief to the appellants. It was June 1980, 2½ years after Oregon's restrictive insanity supervision system had been enacted, before the court of appeals first gave true relief to an appellant. The defendant had been acquitted by insanity of a charge of stealing an automobile. The trial court found the defendant presented a "substantial danger to himself and others" and committed him to the state hospital under the jurisdiction of the PSRB. The court of appeals reversed the trial court order and released the defendant altogether (7).

The court concluded that the evidence of the defendant's sleeping in unlocked cars was insufficient to show dangerousness, absent evidence of violent tendencies against others. The court went on to note that there was substantial evidence to show that the defendant was in need of psychiatric treatment and might need help providing for his personal needs. However, the court noted that although such findings might justify a civil commitment, they did not justify putting the defendant under the PSRB's jurisdiction. The court had established the first limitation on the wide sweep of Oregon's new insanity defense system.

Several months later, the court of appeals discussed a PSRB revocation of conditional release (8). The defendant was diagnosed as having chronic schizophrenia. The trial court found the defendant not guilty by reason of insanity on charges of rape and sodomy, and placed him under the Board's jurisdiction. The Board eventually placed the defendant on conditional release, but revoked him for violating conditions of release. The court concluded that the evidence was insufficient to show that the defendant was ineligible for continued conditional release, although it said that the Board did not have to release him again until suitable arrangements were made for his supervision and treatment. The case is notable for the court's discussion of one aspect of the statutory basis for PSRB jurisdiction. A person may be kept under PSRB supervision even if he or she does not presently present a danger, if the person is "affected by a mental disease or defect in remission . . . [if] the disease may, with reasonable medical probability, occasionally become active and, when active, render the person a danger to others" (9). The court said that the evidence must show a probability of renewed danger in the future, not just a possibility. But the court expressed no problem with the standard itself, even though one might have expected some constitutional concerns about the use of future dangerousness to retain jurisdiction over persons not presently dangerous.

At the end of 1980, the Oregon Supreme Court decided its first PSRB case (10). The trial court found the defendant not guilty of murder by reason of insanity and placed her under the PSRB. The Board held an initial hearing and committed the defendant to the hospital. The defendant challenged the Board's order on several bases, including a claim that the statute deprived her of due process by requiring her to prove that she was no longer dangerous before she could be discharged by the Board, rather than requiring the state to prove she still was dangerous. In this first opportunity to look at the constitutionality of the PSRB system, the Oregon Supreme Court upheld the Board on other grounds without reaching the due process issue.

Thus, when the legislature convened in the spring of 1981 to conduct its sunset review of the PSRB, the new system had survived its first 3 years of operation legally unscathed.

The 1981 Legislative Amendments

Unless renewed by the legislature, the PSRB system would automatically go out of operation on July 1, 1981. Prompted by the deadline, the Governor's Task Force on Mental Health evaluated the Board's effectiveness and presented its findings to the 1981 Legislative Assembly (11). The Task Force report advocated the continuation of the Board, as did virtually every witness who testified before the legislature. The 1981 Legislative Assembly renewed the Board.

However, during this legislative session, there was substantial debate regarding the continued validity of the insanity defense itself and about the relatively high cost of the PSRB system. The legislature refrained from abolishing or changing the insanity defense and confined its efforts to fine-tuning Oregon's unique system, which had been working effectively.

The legislative debate focused on several concerns including the apparent overcrowding in the Oregon State Hospital forensic psychiatric service wards; public concern that persons asserting the insanity defense escape punishment while continuing to pose a danger to the community; procedural issues in the operation of the PSRB; uncertainty about the proper role of the Division; and the lack of definitive statutory or case law standards for key terms such as "mental disease or defect" and "substantial danger." Although the legislature addressed some of these concerns, many of them remained unresolved.

Removal of Certain Misdemeanants From Board Jurisdiction

Under the 1977 statutory scheme, trial judges could place defendants found not responsible because of mental disease or defect under Board jurisdiction upon determining that the defendants continued to have a mental disease or defect and presented a substantial danger to themselves or others (12). In making these determinations, the trial judge was not limited in the evidence that could be considered. Thus, the degree and nature of the crime for which the person was found not responsible was only one factor considered by the judge in determining dangerousness. This meant, for example, that trial court judges placed certain shoplifters under the jurisdiction of the Board because the judges found them to be dangerous, notwithstanding the nondangerous nature of their immediate past crime (13).

Once such an individual arrived at the Oregon State Hospital, however, the hospital staff frequently concluded that the person was not dangerous and that it was an "inappropriate" admission.

As the hospital population continued to increase dramatically, the Division urged the legislature to restrict the pool of persons who could be placed under the Board's jurisdiction. Under the original legislation, only persons who were actually dangerous were to be placed under the jurisdiction of the Board (14). The fact that the Division concluded that a significant number of those placed under the Board's jurisdiction were not dangerous reflected several factors: 1) disagreement as to the meaning of "dangerousness," 2) uncertainty about the quantum of evidence required to prove it, and 3) an apparent stretching of definitions by some trial judges.

At the opening of the 1981 Oregon Legislative Assembly, the Division proposed legislation which would have eliminated PSRB jurisdiction over all persons convicted of any crime, misdemeanor, or felony, not involving violence or the threat of violence (15). After extensive debate, the legislature concluded that this proposal would result in releasing dangerous persons back into the community without controls on them. Testimony indicated that a number of persons found not responsible for nonviolent crimes, such as the unauthorized use of a motor vehicle or forgery, nonetheless had an extensive history of repeated physical violence resulting from mental disease or defect.

However, the legislature did remove the Board's jurisdiction over persons found not responsible due to mental disease or defect for misdemeanors committed during a "criminal episode in the course of which the person did not cause physical injury or risk of physical injury to another" (16). Under the 1981 statutory revision, the trial courts refer these misdemeanants for civil commitment, rather than placing them under Board supervision (17).

This procedure highlighted the difference in burdens of proof utilized in PSRB hearings (a preponderance of the evidence) compared with civil commitments (clear and convincing evidence). Shortly after the 1981 legislative session, the Oregon Court of Appeals upheld the constitutionality of a preponderance burden in commitments by the Board (18). The defendant based her argument on *Addington v. Texas*, (19) in which the U.S. Supreme Court held that in civil commitment proceedings due process requires that the minimum standard of proof be clear and convincing evidence. The defendant contended that her continued criminal commitment by the Board based on the statutory standard of preponderance of the evidence (20) violated due process and equal protection. The Oregon Court of Appeals rejected her argument, reasoning that "there are material distinctions between the two types of proceedings which justify not imposing the same standard of proof. An insanity acquittee has been found by a trier of fact to have engaged in criminal conduct which has threatened public safety and order."

Removal of Those Dangerous Only to Self From PSRB Jurisdiction

The 1981 Legislative Assembly also modified the existing statutes so as to eliminate from placement under the Board's jurisdiction those defendants who, following the finding of not responsible, continue to be affected by mental disease or defect but present a substantial danger only to themselves (21). Furthermore, these individuals were not to be diverted to civil commitment as were the nonviolent misdemeanants, but were to be discharged totally from further supervision (22).

This represented a major philosophical change: the Board was no longer in the business of protecting people from themselves. Yet the practical effect of this change has been minimal. Testimony before the legislative committees indicated that fewer than 5% of those under Board jurisdiction were found to be dangerous only to themselves. Considering that during the first 3 years of the Board's existence trial courts placed an average of 100 persons under its jurisdiction each year, this change eliminated only three or four individuals per year from the Board's jurisdiction and consequently from the state hospital population.

Interestingly, five persons under the Board's jurisdiction in its first years committed suicide. Thus, although the 1981 Legislative Assembly concluded that the Board was not intended to serve a paternalistic function, but rather one of protecting society, experience indicates that many of those under the Board's jurisdiction exhibit extremely self-destructive behavior.

Notification of Victims

In keeping with the overriding concern for protecting victims, the legislature adopted a notification requirement. Upon placing an individual under the jurisdiction of the Board, the trial court must make specific findings on whether there is a victim of the crime and, if so, whether the victim wishes to be notified of any PSRB hearings concerning the defendant and of any conditional release, discharge, or escape of the defendant (23).

Timing of Hearings

In the original 1977 legislation, the statutes required the Board to hold a first hearing within 20 days after the commitment of a person to the state hospital (24). The Division was unable in most instances to develop any kind of conditional release plan for an individual within 20 days. Even for a number of people who could be maintained on conditional release, the initial hearing came and went without any opportunity for their release. As a result, they were usually hospitalized for at least another 6 months until they could apply for a second hearing. Further, the original statute did not provide explicitly for conditional release by the trial court simultaneous with placing a person under the Board's jurisdiction. Furthermore, in *State v. Cooper* (25), the court of appeals held that no appeal lay from the trial court's decision to place a person under the Board's jurisdiction. Rather, the patient had to wait until after the initial hearing of the Board to appeal a denial of conditional release or discharge.

The 1979 Legislative Assembly attempted to remedy these problems by providing explicitly that the trial court could place a person on conditional release (26); that a decision not to release or discharge the person was a final, appealable order (27); and that the initial hearing of the Board was not required until 6 months after commitment (28). The purpose of the changes was to allow the trial court and attorneys familiar with the situation to develop a conditional release plan at the outset. If this were done adequately, then the person would never have to be hospitalized. If an adequate plan could not be formulated at the trial court level, one probably could not be developed within 20 days. Thus, amended legislation gave the hospital up to 6 months to develop a plan. The 1981 legislature shortened this period to 90 days, which they concluded was still long enough so that at the time of the initial hearing, the Board would have something of substance to consider.

Other Procedural Changes

The legislature made a variety of changes in the procedure for handling those people under the jurisdiction of the Board. Several of the legislative changes were an attempt to improve the conditional release process. The new legislation required the Board to hold hearings for conditional release of a patient within 60 days of receiving an application for conditional release accompanied by a "verified" release plan (29). If such an application does not arrive in a timely manner, the Board may request that the Division prepare a predischarge or preconditional release plan for presentation to the Board.

Importantly, the 1981 legislature authorized the Division to contract with public agencies and private corporations other than community mental health programs to provide supervision or treatment for conditionally released people. This change provided a greater number of options for conditional release.

Although the 1981 Legislative Assembly made many changes in the statutes, the major issues surrounding the insanity defense and the Board were left untouched. For example, basic questions concerning the meaning of "mental disease or defect" and "substantial danger" were left unanswered. These terms are not statutorily defined, except that ORS 161.295(2) excludes from "mental disease or defect" abnormalities manifested only by repeated criminal or antisocial conduct (30). Similarly, virtually no case law exists that helps in formulating precise definitions. Instead, the courts joined the legislature in abdicating responsibility for developing definitions of these statutory terms by deferring to "expert" opinions by psychiatrists or psychologists.

The problem is that the exact terms "mental disease or defect" and "substantial danger" are not part of psychiatric or psychological nomenclature; thus, experts are free to interpret these legal terms in light of their professional beliefs. Without guidance from the legislature, the courts, or the medical and psychological sciences, there is a lack of uniformity and predictability in the application of these terms. This uncertainty leads to situations in which two psychiatrists testifying before the Board give identical medical diagnoses of a patient, but one concludes that the condition constitutes "a mental disease or defect" and the other concludes it does not.

The lack of accepted definitions of these statutory terms encourages unseemly battles of experts in court, inconsistency of findings between judges and major disagreements about how many of the commitments to the Board's jurisdiction are "inappropriate." The Governor's Task Force proposed that the Board write such definitions in the form of administrative rules. However, the legislature did not include such a requirement, apparently concluding that this was not a proper task for such a Board. Until either the legislature or the courts accept the responsibility for creating such definitions, this area will remain a major source of confusion and inconsistency in the application of the insanity defense and its sequelae.

Similarly, the legislature failed to designate an appropriate role for members of this unique Board. In an opinion at the end of 1981 (31), the court of appeals addressed this issue. The Board's order had included memoranda by two of its expert members explaining why they decided to continue a defendant under the Board's jurisdiction. The court concluded that portions of these memoranda constituted an impermissible introduction of new evidence, not on the record. Noting that the statutes required that the Board members represent various areas of expertise, the majority of the en banc court of appeals nevertheless precluded the Board from using its "special knowledge as a substitute for evidence presented at a hearing." In a strongly worded dissent, four members of the court asserted that the majority's view would effectively destroy the utility of the expert, professional members of the Board—or at best, force them into undesirable subterfuges. The dissenters went so far as to indicate that, were they expert members of the Board, they would resign, because the majority opinion would so severely and unreasonably limit their ability to perform their appointed duties.

MATURATION OF THE PSRB SYSTEM: 1982–1992

The 1981 legislative actions established the PSRB as an integral part of Oregon's criminal justice system. The next decade saw only a handful of legislative changes, although three 1983 amendments were particularly noteworthy. First, the legislature changed the name of the defense to "guilty except for insanity." This new terminology did not reflect any change in the defense. The legislature's motive was primarily an attempt to help the public better understand that an insanity acquittal was not a finding that the defendant did not do the crime. The misleading nature of the term "not guilty by reason of insanity" was highlighted by the fact that the trial court found Mr. Hinckley, who obviously tried to kill President Reagan, "not guilty." The Oregon Supreme Court discussed this terminology change in a 1990 case, holding that a person charged with a strict liability offense requiring no culpable mental state (such as driving while intoxicated) may raise the insanity defense (32). The court discussed the finding of "guilty except for insanity" and stated:

> In making that change, the legislature understood that the new terminology recognizes even more explicitly that a defendant who is found guilty except for insanity has committed all elements of the crime, although the defendant is to be treated differently at the dispositional stage of the proceedings . . . the defense applies after all elements of the crime have been proved; those elements do not always include a culpable mental state.

The second notable change in 1983 was a new section of the statutes requiring trial judges to advise juries in insanity cases about the PSRB system so that juries would not be under the misperception that a finding of guilty except for insanity meant that a defendant necessarily would be set free and not confined or supervised (33). This statutory addition, like the section that directs PSRB to have its "primary concern the protection of society," (34) is another unusual aspect of Oregon's insanity statutes. They are designed to be straightforward recognitions of the reality of the insanity defense.

The third significant change made by the 1983 legislature was the first—and, so far, only—substantive amendment to the insanity test itself since 1971. The ALI formulation used by Oregon had defined "mental disease or defect" to exclude abnormalities manifested only by repeated criminal or otherwise antisocial conduct. The 1983 legislature added that mental disease or defect also was not to include "any abnormality constituting solely a personality disorder" (35).

This provision was designed to limit the insanity defense to those with major mental diseases or disorders such as psychosis, major affective disorders, organic brain disease, or severe retardation (see Chapter 8). Of course, the statutory phrase did not define personality disorder, thereby leaving much room for disagreement. An Oregon Supreme Court decision in the fall of 1992 illustrated the murkiness of the standard (36). The trial court had placed the defendant under PSRB after finding him guilty except for insanity of kidnapping and assault. Two years later, the defendant sought discharge from PSRB jurisdiction on the grounds that he did not have a mental disease or defect because his condition was best characterized as a personality disorder. The evidence in the record was mixed, with experts giving conflicting conclusions about whether the defendant's acknowledged disorders constituted mental diseases or defects. The court found the evidence insufficient, but remanded the case to PSRB to see if there was additional evidence. The court's discussion of the facts did little to clarify the meaning of the statutory definitions.

However, another case was helpful in defining the reach of the PSRB net. The court of appeals held that an alcoholic individual with permanent brain damage could not be found dangerous and placed under PSRB jurisdiction merely because a psychiatrist testified that alcoholic patients become irritable and angry (37). The court noted that the mere desirability of institutionalization for the defendant's condition is insufficient for commitment under the statute. The fact that a trial court had tried to make such commitment illustrates the lengths to which some judges have sought to stretch the insanity statutes to ensure treatment for some defendants.

Two other cases have addressed fundamental issues surrounding the insanity defense itself. In 1984, the court of appeals held that there was no authority in the Oregon statutes for the court to raise the insanity defense over the objection of the defendant (38). The state charged the defendant with burglary and introduced psychiatric evidence to show he did not have the intent to steal and therefore should be found guilty only of a lesser offense. The prosecutor successfully urged the trial court to find that the defendant was not responsible for burglary because of mental disease or defect. The court of appeals reversed the conviction, saying that it was immaterial whether defendant was "competent" to waive an insanity defense; regardless of his competency, the defendant alone could choose whether or not to raise the defense.

The other noteworthy case involving the defense was a 1991 decision in which the Oregon Supreme Court held that the insanity defense and the defense of extreme emotional disturbance are not mutually exclusive (39). This case reaffirmed the basic nature of the defense: Before responsibility becomes an issue, the prosecution must prove beyond a reasonable doubt that the defendant committed a crime, including all of its elements. By the same token, the defense is entitled to raise any defenses available to show that the defendant did not commit the crime charged, or committed only a lesser one. Thus, the defendant may try to show he did not do the acts charged, he did not have the requisite mental state, or he is "guilty" of only a lesser crime because of extreme emotional disturbance or some other partial defense. Only after all of those issues are raised does the insanity defense come into play.

Although the insanity test employed at trial raises important legal and policy issues, the heart of the PSRB system is the postverdict mechanism for supervising insanity acquittees. Supervision of dangerous offenders creates potential liability for those providing the supervision. However, perhaps because there have been relatively few injuries caused by defendants while under the PSRB, there has been only one significant Oregon appellate decision concerning PSRB-related civil liability.

In 1986, the Oregon Supreme Court heard a wrongful death case brought by a personal representative of a man killed when his automobile was struck by a defendant under PSRB jurisdiction (40). The trial court had found the defendant not responsible because of insanity for crimes arising from a high-speed automobile chase. The trial court placed him under the PSRB. Following a period of hospitalization, the Board placed the defendant on conditional release under the supervision of a private psychiatric day treatment program, which provided services to the PSRB via contract. Although the defendant received intensive monitoring and therapy, he eventually missed an appointment and 2 days later drove 70 miles per hour in a 35-mph zone, ran two red lights, and collided with the decedent's car.

The decedent's representative claimed that, among other things, the day treatment program was negligent in allowing the defendant to drive. The day treatment program contended that it had no legal duty to protect the decedent. The Oregon Supreme Court ruled that the program did have a duty—the PSRB statutes gave community mental health programs authority to take patients back into custody to protect members of the public, and the statutes specified that protection of the public was the primary aim of the PSRB system. The court sent the case to trial so that a jury could decide whether the day treatment program had been negligent in discharging its duty to the decedent. The parties settled the case before trial.

The specter of liability raised by this case has not noticeably chilled the willingness of community mental health programs to provide services for PSRB patients. The conditional release programs continue to be the linchpin of the PSRB system.

CONCLUSION

Oregon's PSRB system retains the legal lines between convictions and insanity verdicts but blurs the practical distinctions. A person found guilty except for insanity in Oregon will likely be confined and supervised longer and more closely, with fewer procedural safeguards, than a person found guilty of the identical crime. The PSRB system has effectively converted Oregon's insanity defense into an "insanity sentence." Such a system would seem to be fertile ground for lawyers and legislators concerned about civil liberties.

However, after some intense legislative scrutiny in its first years, PSRB has been left intact by the legislature, except for minor modifications to clarify and strengthen its role. Apparently, legislators have concluded that the system is succeeding in its primary role of increasing public safety.

Perhaps more surprisingly, the PSRB system has remained largely free of judicially imposed restrictions. Although some lawyers have challenged aspects of the system, the courts have rejected—or ducked—most of those challenges. Given the judicial tenor of the 1990s, it is likely that future challenges will also fail.

The future of the PSRB will rest more on politics and economics than on legal issues. The PSRB has become an established and accepted part of Oregon's legal framework.

REFERENCES

1. Treleaven JH: Facts, impressions, hypotheses, problems, and recommendations related to management of persons found not guilty of a crime due to mental disease or defect (Jan. 15, 1976) (unpublished report)

2. Colbach: Insanity defense is indefensible. Willamette Week, November 3, 1975, at 9, col. I

3. Report of the Governor's Task Force on Corrections: A Community Corrections System for Oregon (Sept. 1976) (revised Oct. 1976)

4. Oregon Revised Statutes §161.385 (1977) amended by, 1979 Or. Laws, ch. 885

5. State v Cooper, 37 Or. App. 443, 587 P.2d 1051 (1978)

6. Cardwell v Psychiatric Security Review Board, 38 Or. App. 565, 590 P.2d 787 (1978), *rev dismissed* 286 Or. 521 (1979)

7. State v Rath, 46 Or. App. 695, 613 P.2d 60 (1980)

8. Cochenour v PSRB, 47 Or. App. 1097, 615 P.2d 1155 (1980)

9. Oregon Revised Statutes §161.333(3)

10. Adams v PSRB, 290 Or. 273, 621 P.2d 572 (1980)

11. Governor's Task Force on Mental Health: Sunset Review of the Psychiatric Security Review Board, December, 1980

12. Oregon Revised Statutes §161.336 (1977) (amended by 1979 Or. Laws, ch. 885)

13. See Minutes of Hearings on H.B. 2410 Before the Or. House Comm. on the Judiciary, Subcomm. 3, 61st Legislative Assembly, Exhibit B (Mar. 2, 1981) (letter of Jan. 26, 1981 from J. H. Treleaven, M.D., Assistant Director, Human Resources, Administrator for Mental Health, to The Honorable Jan Wyers, Chairperson, Senate Comm. on Justice, presented by J. D. Bray, M.D., Assistant Administrator, Programs for Mental or Emotional Disturbances)

14. Oregon Revised Statutes §161.327

15. See Minutes of Hearings on S.B. 167 Before the Senate Comm. on Justice, 61st Or. Legislation Assembly, Exhibit D (Feb. 4, 1981) (memorandum letter from J. H. Treleaven, M.D., Assistant Director, Human Resources, Administrator for Mental Health, to The Honorable Jan Wyers, Chairperson, Senate Comm. on Justice, presented by J. D. Bray, M.D., Assistant Administrator, Programs for Mental or Emotional Disturbances)

16. 1981 Or. Laws, ch. 711, §3

17. 1981 Or. Laws, ch. 711, §3(2)

18. Ashley v PSRB, 59 Or. App. 333, 632 P.2d 15 (1981)

19. 441 US 418 (1979)

20. According to Oregon Revised Statutes §161.346(9), "The burden of proof on all issues at hearings of the board shall be by a preponderance of the evidence."

21. 1981 Or. Laws, ch. 711, §4 (amending ORS 161.329)

22. 1981 Or. Laws, ch. 711, §4

23. 1981 Or. Laws, ch. 711, §I (adding §2(b) to ORS 161.325)

24. Oregon Revised Statutes §161.336(1)

25. State v Cooper, 37 Or. App. 443, 587 P.2d 1051 (1978)

26. Oregon Revised Statutes §161.327(2)(b)

27. Oregon Revised Statutes §161.327(7)

28. Oregon Revised Statutes §161.341(1)

29. 1981 Or. Laws, ch. 711, §6 (amending ORS 161.341)

30. Oregon Revised Statutes §161.295(2)

31. Rolfe v PSRB, 53 Or. App. 941, 948-51, 633 P.2d 846, *rev den* 292 Or. 334 (1981)

32. State v Olmstead, 310 Or. 455, 800 P.2d 277 (1990)

33. 1983 Or. Laws, ch. 800, §16

34. Oregon Revised Statutes §161.336(10)

35. Oregon Revised Statutes §161.295

36. Martin v PSRB, 312 Or. 157, 818 P.2d 1264 (1991)

37. State v LeHuquet, 54 Or. App. 895, 636 P.2d 467 (1981)

38. State v Peterson, 70 Or. App. 333, 689 P.2d 985 (1984)
39. State v Counts, 311 Or. 616, 816 P.2d 1157 (1991)
40. Cain v Rijken, 300 Or. 706, 717 P.2d 140 (1986)

Chapter 3

Who Are Oregon's Insanity Acquittees?

In this chapter, we describe the characteristics of Oregon's insanity acquittees *at the time of assignment to the Psychiatric Security Review Board (PSRB)*, with particular attention to their prior involvement with the mental health and criminal justice systems. In 1983, Steadman and Braff (1) formulated a research agenda regarding the insanity defense that, in part, focused on the characteristics and possible treatment of insanity acquittees. They stated:

> . . . in developing appropriate programs for NGRIs [individuals found not guilty by reason of insanity], standard models for prisoners or mental patients both are inappropriate. They may be a class unto themselves. Like much else about the insanity acquittee, these possible program implications are quite speculative. There is simply insufficient descriptive information about acquittees' demographic, criminal and mental hospital history, and current clinical characteristics from which rational program development can proceed.

As will be seen from our discussion in this chapter, considerable progress has been made in shedding light on the question of the involvement of Oregon's insanity acquittees in the mental health systems and criminal justice systems.

The data presented here and in most of the subsequent chapters in this book derive from a recently completed study funded by the National Institute of Mental Health (2), which allowed us to develop in-depth information on a group of individuals assigned to the PSRB between 1978 and 1986. The overall project was designed to study the demographic characteristics of Oregon's insanity acquittees, their past involvements with the mental health and criminal justice systems, their management while under the jurisdiction of the PSRB (including the treatment they received while on conditional release), and their subsequent involvement with the mental health and criminal justice systems following discharge from PSRB jurisdiction.

We begin with a brief description of research methodology and how we developed the cohort of 758 individuals that forms the core sample for most of the data presented in this book. Subsequent chapters investigate subpopulations primarily derived from this sample.

RESEARCH METHODOLOGY

Most of the material for this book derives from six operational data bases, each of which is described briefly in this section.

PSRB Research Data Base

Since the PSRB was first implemented on January 1, 1978, we have maintained a data base on all individuals under the Board's jurisdiction. The data base contains limited demographic and diagnostic information, a record of the criminal charge that resulted in the subjects' assignments to the PSRB, and the maximum length of PSRB jurisdiction on all individuals placed under the Board's jurisdiction. We update the data base yearly. In addition to adding new cases to the file, these updates document all major Board actions that result in changes in placement (e.g., when an individual is conditionally released from the forensic hospital to the community, or when a conditional release is revoked and the individual is returned to the forensic hospital). We record the date of each Board action and are able to calculate the length of time in each placement. Finally, we record discharges and the reason for the discharge.

Mental Health Data Base

The Mental Health Information System (MHIS) is a computerized statewide hospital and community mental health case register that the Oregon Mental Health and Developmental Disabilities Services Division (the Division) maintains. We extracted data on mental health service utilization for all individuals assigned to the PSRB from 1978 through 1986, the end of the study period. These data include inpatient mental health episodes in the three Oregon state hospitals and outpatient treatment episodes from community mental health programs. Data collection focused on three time periods: prior to PSRB placement, during PSRB jurisdiction, and following PSRB jurisdiction for those individuals discharged during our study period.

This data base contains extensive information on utilization of state mental health services, including voluntary and involuntary hospitalizations and use of community services. The hospital portion of the MHIS includes information dating to 1950; however, it is most reliable from the 1970s to the present. Community service data were not reliably documented until 1980 or 1981. Since then, community service data were recorded by service elements, such as outpatient services, residential services, precommitment services, and PSRB community services.

An additional limitation in our data regarding the mental health service utilization of this population derives from the fact that MHIS has no information from Oregon's community hospitals or from private mental health providers and has no service utilization data from other states. As a result of these limitations, the information on mental health services reported in this book represents a conservative depiction of the services received by these subjects.

Criminal Justice Data Base

This data base contains information on all individuals assigned to the PSRB from 1978 through 1986 and is also structured in the three time periods described above. We constructed the criminal justice data base from three computerized law enforcement data systems: a statewide system, a system covering the three counties constituting the Portland metropolitan area, and a federal system. From these systems, we extracted the total number of police contacts prior to, during, and following PSRB jurisdiction, as well as more detailed information for as many as 10 separate contacts prior to PSRB, 5 contacts during PSRB, and 5 contacts following PSRB jurisdiction. These detailed blocks of information included the nature of the police contact, the date, and the location of the contact. It is important to note that these data represent contacts only and not convictions and subsequent dispositions. Our data allow for these additions in the future but are not reported here.

We believe that the data from these three criminal justice data bases also reflect a conservative estimate of the amount of contact that the subjects in this study had with the criminal justice system. For example, we found that records for a small number of subjects did not reflect the crime leading to PSRB jurisdiction, suggesting an underreporting of criminal contacts.

The Crime Seriousness Score

Multiple charges may have resulted from an individual's contact with the police, and we recorded each of these charges. However, to simplify reporting, we identified the single most serious charge for each incident. The hierarchy of seriousness of crimes was based on a rating system that we had developed for an earlier study (3). This rating system ranks crimes within the Oregon statutory scheme according to the class of crime, starting with murder, felony murder, and conspiracy murder and then Class A Felonies through Class C Misdemeanors, followed by violations such as parole or probation violations and traffic infractions. Then, within each class, we ranked crimes according to the seriousness of the crime using the following two general guidelines. We ranked crimes against the person as more serious than crimes against property, and we ranked completed crimes as more serious than attempted or inchoate crimes. Once we had completed the ranking, we divided 100 points between the crimes in each class, starting from 100–199 for the class of murders to 700–799 for Class C Misdemeanors. We assigned the noncriminal violations a score of 850. The murder class contains only three crimes, so there is a wide spread between the crimes; the largest classes are Class C Felonies ($n = 41$) and Class A Misdemeanors ($n = 55$), with a small point spread between crimes.

PSRB Record Data Base

There were 381 subjects on conditional release at some point during the 1978–1986 study period. For these subjects, we gathered data from records maintained by the PSRB. We were primarily interested in the supervision and treatment information contained in the reporting forms that the community programs submit monthly to the PSRB on conditionally released subjects.

Community Program Record Data Base

To get an in-depth view of the treatment offered to subjects on conditional release, we conducted a chart review of treatment records for a group of male subjects the courts assigned to PSRB jurisdiction as a result of a felony charge, whom state hospital personnel diagnosed as psychotic, and who spent time on conditional release in one of the three largest community treatment programs ($n = 93$). We extracted detailed information from these community treatment records on the mental health services received by these subjects during the time that they were in these programs, including mental health, medical, social support, vocational, residential, and other support services.

Community Interview Data Base

The final data base focused on the adjustment and quality of life of a small group of conditionally released subjects whom we interviewed every 3 months for a 2-year period. We again chose males, assigned to PSRB jurisdiction as a result of a felony crime, diagnosed as psychotic, and on conditional release in one of the three largest community treatment programs. We developed a sample of 54 subjects whom we interviewed, along with their case managers, every 2 months during this 2-year period. This data base includes information from a number of measures. The subject interviews generated detailed information on quality of life, mental health history, current symptomatology, and compliance with treatment programs. In addition to these semi-structured interviews, we used a number of standardized instruments, including the Mini-Mental State Exam, the Hopkins

Symptom Checklist—90 (SCL-90), and portions of the Schedule for Affective Disorders and Schizophrenia (SADS), Lifetime and Change versions. The case manager interview focused on key areas of client adjustment, such as compliance with treatment programs and symptom management.

We were also interested in the question of revocation. During the 2-year study period there were 16 revocations among the 54 subjects who made up this sample. Following a revocation, we interviewed both the subject and the case manager to determine the reasons for revocation and assess the subject's symptomatology at the time of revocation.

THE SAMPLE

Between 1978 and 1986, the court placed 971 individuals under the jurisdiction of the PSRB. To arrive at our core research sample, we excluded the 152 individuals who raised successful insanity defenses in the years prior to the initiation of the PSRB and whom the courts transferred to the Board's jurisdiction when it began operation on January 1, 1978. We excluded these individuals because we have found, in previous studies, that they have consistently demonstrated some characteristics significantly different from those of individuals who entered the system after the PSRB began functioning on January 1, 1978. This is most likely explained by the fact that these pre-1978 subjects represented those individuals remaining under state supervision from the totality of those found not guilty by reason of insanity in the years prior to 1978. In contrast, we have data on all of the insanity acquittees committed to the Board's jurisdiction after 1978. Because there was a danger that the pre-1978 sample could distort the overall findings, we excluded these subjects from the core research sample.

We also excluded individuals who displayed unusual histories while under PSRB jurisdiction, including those who served their PSRB time in correctional facilities ($n = 2$), those who were placed out of state ($n = 2$), those who were lost to PSRB monitoring ($n = 14$), and the one individual who was deported. There were 38 individuals who had multiple PSRB episodes in the study period. For these individuals, we examined data only from the first assignment to PSRB jurisdiction. This was done so that we could present our data in terms of individuals rather than episodes of assignment to PSRB jurisdiction.

OREGON'S INSANITY ACQUITTEES AT THE TIME OF COMMITMENT TO THE PSRB

We were left with a research sample of 758 individuals. Entry of subjects into the system was fairly equally divided across the 9-year time period. The courts committed subjects to the jurisdiction of the PSRB from 33 of Oregon's 36 counties. Courts in three very sparsely populated rural counties failed to commit an individual to the jurisdiction of the Board during the 1978–1986 study period.

In 1984, Oregon had a population of 2,660,000 people (4). On a statewide basis, judges committed 28 acquittees per 100,000 population. The 5 most populous counties accounted for 58% of the state's population and produced 67% of the state's insanity acquittees. As depicted in Table 3–1, we compared the distribution of insanity acquittees with Oregon's population in eight of Oregon's counties illustrated in the table. We found that courts in 3 of Oregon's 5 most populous counties committed more insanity acquittees than the average of 28 per 100,000, whereas courts in the 2 other counties committed fewer acquittees. For example, the city of Portland is located in Multnomah County, which is Oregon's most populous county. This county had a rate of 39 per

Table 3–1.   Assignment to the PSRB by county

County	Population	PSRB	Rate per 100,000
Multnomah	561,800	218	39
Lane	269,500	135	50
Washington	268,000	30	11
Clackamas	248,200	37	15
Marion	209,200	83	40
Statewide	2,660,000	758	28

100,000 compared with Washington County, which had a rate of 11 per 100,000.

Demographics

Eighty-six percent of the sample were men and 14% were women. The mean age was 32, with an age range from 17 to 83. Fifty percent of the sample were between ages 20 and 30 at the time of assignment to the PSRB. The following demographic information comes from the MHIS. Although data are not available on all subjects for all reported variables, there is no reason to believe that there is systematic bias in relation to missing data. Eighty-seven percent of the subjects were white and 8% were African American, with the remainder divided among American Indians, Hispanics, and Asians. Forty-eight percent of subjects failed to graduate from high school, and 28% had a high school diploma. Nineteen percent had some college experience, and 3% graduated from college.

Most subjects (59%) were never married, while 29% were either divorced or separated. Only 8% were married. Most subjects (55%) were unemployed when they entered the mental health system. Of those who were employed, 37% were in various types of laboring jobs, with 5% in sheltered workshops. Only 3% of those employed reported occupations that usually require some form of higher education at the technical or managerial level.

Thirty-two percent of the subjects lived alone at the time of their encounter with the mental health system, and 27% were living in some type of protected housing arrangement. Another 22% lived with nuclear family, while 16% lived with a spouse or friend.

Diagnosis

We were able to look at the diagnoses made of each individual at several points in time. We compared the available diagnoses to categorize subjects into mutually exclusive diagnostic categories. Schizophrenia was the most prevalent diagnosis. We categorized subjects as schizophrenic if they had been diagnosed with schizophrenia or schizoaffective disorder in at least 50% of the instances where a diagnosis was available, and if they never were diagnosed as mentally retarded or as having an organic mental disorder. To obtain a single working diagnosis, we categorized the remaining subjects using the following hierarchy: mental retardation, organic mental disorder, psychosis, personality disorder, other disorder, and substance abuse disorder. The "other disorder" category includes several individuals with pedophilia, sexual conduct disorder, factitious disorder, anxiety disorder, or depressive disorder.

Following these rules, diagnoses are reported in Table 3–2. As can be seen, schizophrenia was the single largest diagnostic category, accounting for 60% of the sample. This was followed by personality disorder, bipolar disorder, and other psychosis. Substance abuse disorders, as a primary diagnosis, accounted for only 3% of the subjects in this sample. However, we found that 27% (*n* = 204) of the sample had substance abuse disorders described in the records we reviewed.

Table 3–2. Lifetime diagnoses of PSRB subjects (*N* = 697)

Diagnosis	*n*	%
Psychosis	499	72
Schizophrenia	421	60
Bipolar disorder	46	7
Other psychosis	32	5
Personality disorder (PD)	75	11
Antisocial PD	23	3
Borderline PD	12	2
Schizoid PD	9	1
Paranoid PD	8	1
Inadequate PD	7	1
Passive-aggressive PD	5	1
Other PD	11	2
Mental retardation	56	8
Organic mental disorder	32	5
Substance abuse disorder only	21	3
Other disorder	14	2

Prior Use of State Hospitals and Community
Mental Health Services

As we mentioned, the MHIS contains information on both state hospital and community mental health service data. Hospital data are presented in Table 3–3. Seventy-seven percent of the sample had had a state hospitalization at some point prior to commitment to the PSRB. Subjects had a mean of 3.1 prior hospitalizations, with a range of 0 to 22, and had spent a mean of 454 days in hospital prior to PSRB commitment. Most of these hospital episodes (59%) were involuntary. Nine percent of the subjects experienced only voluntary hospitalization at some point prior to PSRB commitment.

We were particularly interested in the time period immediately prior to entry into the PSRB. We examined hospitalization data for the 2 years prior to commitment to PSRB. Sixty-nine percent of subjects were hospitalized in this 2-year period of time, spending a mean of 85 days per subject in a state hospital. Sixty-eight percent of these hospital episodes were involuntary.

The data from the community mental health system were limited by the fact that adequate reporting for community service episodes dates to 1981. At that time, community mental health programs were refocused on chronic mentally ill people (see Chapter 1). To get meaningful community service data, we

Table 3–3.   State hospital utilization prior to the PSRB (*N* = 758)

	Voluntary hospital episodes		Involuntary hospital episodes		Total	
	n	%	*n*	%	*n*	%
No. episodes						
0	460	61	225	30	175	23
1	133	18	209	28	184	24
2–5	112	15	273	36	268	35
> 5	53	7	51	7	131	17
Mean	1.3		1.8		3.1	
SD	2.72		2.24		4.15	
Range	0–22		0–17		0–28	
Mean number of days	81		303		454	

looked at a cohort of 302 subjects who entered the system between 1983 and 1986. We found that 227 (75%) received some community mental health services in the 2 years prior to entry into the PSRB. If we combine hospital and community services for these 302 subjects, 259 (86%) received services. On average, these individuals were registered as active patients, either in the hospital or in community programs, for 34% of the days in this 2-year period.

Criminal Justice System Contacts

The trial courts assigned 73% of the sample to the PSRB following charges involving felony crimes, and 27% following charges of misdemeanor crimes. Table 3–4 presents the maximum length of assignment of subjects to PSRB jurisdiction. This period is determined by the maximum sentence that the courts could have imposed if the individual had been found guilty of the crimes charged. Courts may assign individuals with multiple charges to the Board's jurisdiction for longer periods reflecting consecutive sentencing. Thus, although courts assigned 27% of the sample to PSRB jurisdiction as a result of misdemeanor charges, 25% had sentences of 1 year or less. The remaining subjects assigned following misdemeanor offenses are included in the 5-year category in the table as a result of multiple misdemeanor charges. Courts assigned 20 (2.6%) subjects to PSRB jurisdiction for life, representing those assigned for murder charges.

Table 3–5 summarizes the crimes leading to PSRB jurisdiction and the criminal contacts of this group prior to PSRB jurisdiction.

Table 3–4. Length of assignment to PSRB jurisdiction (N = 758)

Length of assignment	n	%
1 year	189	25
5 years	240	32
10 years	115	15
20 years	170	22
40+ years	24	3
Life	20	3

The most frequently occurring felonies were assaults, burglaries and unauthorized use of motor vehicles. Courts committed 32 of the 53 subjects in the homicide category to PSRB jurisdiction following homicide charges. Of these, 20 were murder cases and 12 were manslaughter cases. Cases resulting in the death of another individual accounted for 4% of the crimes that led to PSRB jurisdiction. Menacing/harassment was the most frequently occurring misdemeanor. The mean seriousness score of the crime leading to PSRB jurisdiction was 401 (SD = 128).

Subjects in this study had extensive involvement with the criminal justice system prior to assignment to the PSRB, with a mean number of 5.5 police contacts per subject. To focus on those contacts related to crimes, we excluded categories of noncriminal contacts including parole or probation violations (n = 63), contacts related to mental illness (n = 46), noncriminal juvenile contacts (n = 38), traffic infractions (n = 25), and alcohol- or drug-related contacts (n = 19). After excluding these noncriminal contacts, we found that 77% of the subjects were charged with criminal offenses prior to the crime that led to PSRB jurisdiction. They had an average of 4.05 criminal contacts per person. When we corrected these contacts for time, we found that subjects experienced an average of 0.49 police contacts per adult year (number of contacts per year for each year over age 18).

These prior criminal contacts are depicted in Table 3–5. Forty-seven percent of these prior criminal contacts were for felony crimes, whereas 53% were misdemeanors. Leading past felony contacts were for assaults and burglaries followed by drug-related charges, thefts, and unauthorized use of motor vehicles. There were a small number of homicides, accounting for fewer than 1% of the prior felonies. Leading misdemeanors included theft, driving offenses, menacing and harassment, and trespass. The mean seriousness score of the criminal contacts prior to the index crime leading to PSRB jurisdiction was 432.

Combined Mental Health and Criminal Justice Contacts

To address the question posed by Steadman and Braff regarding the resemblance of insanity acquittees to mental patients and/or to offenders (1), we examined prior contacts with the mental

Table 3–5. Criminal justice contacts (*N* = 758)

	PSRB charge		Prior to PSRB assignment	
	n	%	*n*	%
Felony crimes	554	73	1,170	47
Assault	98	13	192	8
Burglary	81	11	209	8
Unauthorized use of auto	70	9	77	3
Arson	56	7	43	2
Sexual assault	56	7	37	1
Robbery	46	6	85	3
Criminal mischief	30	4	70	3
Murder	22	3	5	< 1
Attempted homicide	19	3	5	< 1
Theft	17	2	124	5
Manslaughter	12	2	—	—
Kidnapping	12	2	10	< 1
Escape/failure to appear	8	1	97	4
Driving offenses	5	1	23	1
Weapons offenses	5	1	3	< 1
Drug offenses	4	1	141	6
Other felony	13	2	49	2
Misdemeanor crimes	204	27	1,313	53
Menacing/harassment	80	11	184	7
Theft	25	3	384	16
Criminal mischief	20	3	59	2
Trespass	19	3	171	7
Sexual offenses	16	2	52	2
Resisting arrest	14	2	128	5
Driving offenses	13	2	200	8
Arson	8	1	8	< 1
Weapons offenses	7	1	45	2
Escape/fail to appear	—	—	52	2
Other misdemeanor	2	< 1	30	1

health and criminal justice systems for the 758 subjects in this study. We excluded the criminal justice contact that led to PSRB jurisdiction. On the mental health side we limited the comparison to previous hospitalizations and eliminated community contacts because of the inconsistency of the reporting of community data in the early years of the study period.

As depicted in Figure 3–1, only 55 subjects (7%) in the sample had no prior contacts with either the mental health or the criminal justice system. Another 120 individuals (16%) had prior contacts with the mental health system and none with criminal justice, and a similar number of 118 subjects (16%) had no prior contact with mental health but did have contacts with criminal justice. Four hundred and sixty-five subjects (61%) had prior contacts with both systems.

There was no significant difference in the number of mental health contacts for those with or without criminal justice contacts and there was also no significant difference in the number of criminal justice contacts for those with or without mental health contacts. Those with criminal justice contacts, whether combined or not with mental health contacts, were significantly younger (i.e., an average age of 31 as compared with 34–35). Women demonstrated significantly fewer criminal justice contacts, either

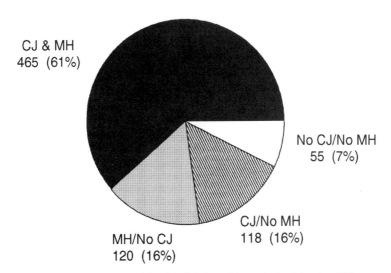

Figure 3–1. Prior mental health (MH) and/or criminal justice (CJ) contacts (PSRB clients 1978–1986; N = 758).

combined or not with mental health contacts (see Chapter 10 for a discussion of women in the system). As expected, schizophrenics were more heavily represented in the mental health system, with more than expected prior contacts, and in the group with combined mental health and criminal justice contacts. They were underrepresented in the groups with no prior contacts or contacts only in the criminal justice system (see Chapter 8 for discussion of diagnosis). Finally, those subjects with documented histories of substance abuse were significantly overrepresented in the groups with criminal justice contacts (χ^2 = 11.042, df = 1, P = .0009).

DISCUSSION

This chapter has described insanity acquittees at the time of their commitment by trial court judges to the jurisdiction of the PSRB. Judges assigned individuals to the PSRB from 33 of Oregon's 36 counties. Courts in these counties committed insanity acquittees to the PSRB at different rates when compared with each county's percentage of the total state population. These findings are similar to previous work in Oregon, related to differential commitment rates in civil commitment in Oregon (5, 6).

At this point we can only speculate about the differential rates of commitment of subjects to the jurisdiction of the PSRB from these counties. We could look for explanations on the criminal justice side of the equation. In this area it would be important to have some measure of how the insanity defense is used in these counties, including measures of arrests, insanity pleas compared with convictions, and insanity verdicts (7). We could also look for explanations on the mental health side, starting with epidemiological differences in the rates of the different mental illnesses in these different counties.

We believe that in four of the five most populous counties, the rate of successful insanity defenses was in the expected direction. The two counties that have lower rates of commitment compared with their general populations were predominantly affluent and suburban.

The three counties in which the courts commit at rates higher than expected included Multnomah County, which is the site of the state's largest city, Portland, and Marion County, the fifth most populous Oregon county. Portland, as the largest city in Oregon, shares many of the problems of large cities across this country, with a large homeless population and a public mental health system strained beyond its capacity to deliver services. Marion County's major city, Salem, is the state capital. Located within its boundaries are two state prisons, the hospital for the mentally retarded, and the large state hospital that houses the forensic psychiatric program, among other inpatient units. One might expect high percentages of seriously mentally ill individuals in the populations of these two counties when compared with most other counties in the state—hence, an increase in the use of the various measures of social control including diversion of individuals to the criminal justice system (8) and the use of the insanity defense.

Lane County had the highest rate of commitment of these five counties (see Table 3-1). It is hard to explain the high rate of successful insanity defenses in this particular county. It is a relatively affluent county with a major state university in its largest city, Eugene. One possible explanation for the higher commitment rate might relate to the presence of this university that, like other similar institutions, attracts a larger proportion of mentally ill individuals who live peripheral to the campus.

Demographically this sample of insanity acquittees appears compatible with previous descriptions in the literature (9–11). It is made up mainly of men, and although the average age is 32, half of the sample is under age 30. In keeping with Oregon's population distribution, the sample is predominantly white. When subjects encountered the mental health system, at various times in their lives, they were predominantly unemployed or underemployed. They lived either alone, with family, or in protected settings. These limited demographic characteristics predominantly define a chronically mentally ill population that is extremely dependent on family and on public services for financial and mental health services.

There was great diversity in the index felony crimes that lead to PSRB jurisdiction, with assaults, burglaries, and unauthorized use of automobile being the most frequently occurring in this sample. Homicides were relatively rare, accounting for only 4% of the felony crimes associated with a successful insanity defense. Oregon also has a sizable number of its insanity acquittees committed following misdemeanor crimes associated with danger to others. This is a controversial group of subjects. There are questions about whether this group of mentally ill individuals represent an appropriate group for an insanity defense or whether they should be diverted to the civil commitment system. This topic is addressed in Chapter 9.

It is important at this point to return to Steadman and Braff's question regarding the characteristics of insanity acquittees (1). The data available to us allow for reasonable characterization of psychiatric diagnosis and the past mental health and criminal justice system involvement of the subjects in this study. Psychosis accounted for 72% of diagnoses. The largest group of subjects (60%) had schizophrenia, with an additional 7% having bipolar disorder. There were three other diagnostic groups with significant representation in this population, including subjects with personality disorders (11%), those with mental retardation (8%), and those with organic mental disorders (5%).

Only 27% of the subjects had substance abuse disorders as a primary or secondary diagnosis. We believe this finding probably represents serious underreporting of concomitant substance abuse in this study population. In an earlier paper (12), we described a group of subjects conditionally released to a large urban treatment program during the first 3 years of the PSRB's operation. In this earlier study, we had more detailed information available and found that 50% of the subjects had a history of substance abuse. Data from the Epidemiologic Catchment Area studies reveal lifetime comorbidity of schizophrenia with substance abuse of 47%, 61% with bipolar disorder, and 84% with antisocial personality disorder (13). Given the demographic and diagnostic characteristics of our study subjects, their involvement in the criminal justice system, and the findings of our previous study, we would have expected much higher rates of reported substance abuse in the study group.

Our data indicate that only 7% of subjects had no involvement with either the mental health or criminal justice system prior to commitment to the jurisdiction of the PSRB. The majority of subjects, 61%, had significant prior experience with both systems. This is in marked contrast to the Missouri study cited earlier (10), in which 28% had prior contact with both the criminal justice and mental health systems.

Seventy-seven percent of the subjects in this sample were in a state hospital at some time prior to their commitment to the PSRB, with a mean of 3.1 prior state hospitalizations per person. These admissions were predominantly involuntary civil commitments. In the years prior to the PSRB, commitment subjects spent an average of 454 days in state hospitals. A recent study from Maryland (14) focused on the involvement of insanity acquittees in the mental health and criminal justice systems before and after their hospitalization as insanity acquittees. The authors found that 59% of their subjects were hospitalized prior to the insanity verdict. Rates of prior hospitalization similar to Oregon's were found in Missouri (10), with 79% of the reported sample demonstrating prior psychiatric history. In a recent study from California (15), 72% of the insanity acquittees studied had prior hospitalizations.

We know of no other reports that describe community mental health system involvement of insanity acquittees prior to their insanity verdict. As we demonstrated from our community mental health services data, 75% of the subjects had been provided with some community mental health service prior to assignment to the PSRB.

On the criminal justice side, 77% of the subjects had prior contacts with the criminal justice system, with an average of 4.05 criminal contacts per subject. From another viewpoint, subjects had an average of 0.49 contacts per year during their adult years. These prior contacts were almost evenly divided between felonies and misdemeanors. In the Missouri study (10), 51% had contact with the criminal justice system prior to their insanity acquittal and hospitalization. Our findings in Oregon are directly comparable with those of the Maryland study (14), in which 76% had prior criminal justice involvement, and to one done in California (15), in which 78% had such involvement. A more recent study from California (16) found rates of prior arrests and prior state hospitalizations almost identical to what is reported in this chapter.

Thus, the typical insanity acquittee in Oregon (and most likely in other jurisdictions) is a male in his mid-30s with a schizophrenic illness, and who has considerable past experience in both the mental health and criminal justice systems. Substance abuse, which we believe is underreported in our data, appears to be an additional important factor related to criminal justice system involvement. The typical subject's past hospitalizations have been more involuntary than voluntary, indicating considerable experience with civil commitment and perhaps an inability on his part to recognize and acknowledge his mental illness.

As is demonstrated later in this book, we believe that there is now enough information about insanity acquittees to foster rational program development both in Oregon and in other jurisdictions. In Oregon, program development has progressed along certain lines that mesh, in a productive manner, with the characteristics of the subjects described in this report. As we described in Chapter 1, the Oregon Legislature developed the PSRB with a primary focus on security, whereas the program development of the Division gradually moved during the past 15 years to a focus on chronically mentally ill people. In the remaining chapters, we focus on the interaction of the PSRB and the Division as their programs and decisions affect the 758 subjects whose careers are the focus of this book.

REFERENCES

1. Steadman HJ, Braff J: Defendants not guilty by reason of insanity, in Mentally Disordered Offenders: Perspectives From Law and Social Science. Edited by Monahan J, Steadman HJ. New York, Plenum, 1983, pp 109–129
2. Management and Treatment of Insanity Acquittees in Oregon, RO1-MH-42221, National Institute of Mental Health, 1986
3. Bloom JD, Rogers JL, Manson SM: After Oregon's insanity defense: a comparison of conditional release and hospitalization. Int J Law Psychiatry 5:391–402,1982
4. Oregon Secretary of State: Oregon Blue Book, 1985–1986. Salem, OR, Oregon Secretary of State, 1985

5. Faulkner LR, Bloom JD, Resnick MR, et al: Local variations in the civil commitment process. Bull Am Acad Psychiatry Law 11:5–17, 1983
6. Faulkner LR, Bloom JD, Stern TO: Rural civil commitment. Bull Am Acad Psychiatry Law 12 359–371, 1984
7. Callahan L, Mayer C, Steadman HJ: Insanity defense reform in the United States post Hinckley. Mental and Physical Disability Law Reporter 11:54–59, 1987
8. Bloom JD, Shore JH, Arvidson B: Local variations in the arrests of psychiatric patients. Bull Am Acad Psychiatry Law 9:203–210, 1981
9. Pasewark RA: Insanity plea: a review of the research literature. Journal of Psychiatry and Law 9:357–402, 1982
10. Petrilla J: The insanity defense and other mental health dispositions in Missouri. Int J Law Psychiatry 5:81–101, 1982
11. Zonana HV, Wells JA, Getz MA, et al: The NGRI registry: initial analyses of data collected on Connecticut insanity acquittees. Bull Am Acad Psychiatry Law 18:115–128, 1990
12. Bloom JD, Williams MH, Rogers JL, et al: Evaluation and treatment of insanity acquittees in the community. Bull Am Acad Psychiatry Law 14:231–244, 1986
13. Reiger DA, Farmer ME, Rae DS, et al: Comorbidity of mental disorders with alcohol and other drug abuse. JAMA 264:2511–2518, 1990
14. Silver SB, Cohen MI, Spodak MK: Follow-up after release of insanity acquittees: mentally disordered offenders and convicted felons. Bull Am Acad Psychiatry Law 17:387–400, 1989
15. Lamb HR, Weinberger LE, Gross BH: Court-mandated community outpatient treatment for persons found Not Guilty by Reason of Insanity: a five-year follow-up. Am J Psychiatry 145:450–456, 1988
16. Wiederanders MR: Recidivism of disordered offenders who were conditionally vs. unconditionally released. Behavioral Sciences and the Law 10:141–148, 1992

Chapter 4

Hospitalization and Conditional Release of Insanity Acquittees

The power to grant and to revoke the conditional release of insanity acquittees is a key feature of the Oregon system for managing these acquittees. As we described in Chapter 1, the Psychiatric Security Review Board (PSRB) governs placement of insanity acquittees in the hospital and community treatment programs, although the Oregon Mental Health and Developmental Disabilities Services Division (the Division) is responsible for the treatment provided to insanity acquittees in the forensic hospital and in community treatment programs. After a finding of "guilty except for insanity," the trial court judge determines if the individual remains mentally ill and dangerous to others; if so, the judge must commit the individual to the jurisdiction of the PSRB. The trial court judge also determines the length of the insanity sentence and makes the initial placement of the individual, either in the forensic hospital or on conditional release in the community.

In a prior study (1), we examined the question of conditional release by focusing on 299 subjects whom the courts placed under PSRB jurisdiction during its first 3 years of operation (1978–1980). We compared three groups of insanity acquittees: 1) those individuals judges placed on conditional release, 2) those individuals judges hospitalized and who spent their entire period under the Board's jurisdiction or the entire study period in the hospital, and 3) those individuals judges hospitalized and whom the Board later placed on conditional release. In this chapter, we repeat and expand on the analyses done for the earlier study with the 9-year sample of 758 subjects who form the core sample for this book.

SYSTEM CHARACTERISTICS

Of the 758 subjects in this study, Oregon judges initially placed 597 (79%) in the forensic hospital and 161 (21%) on conditional release. Once the judges made these initial placements, 377 subjects (67% of those hospitalized) never left the hospital until the Board discharged them or the study period ended. Of the 161 subjects the judges initially placed in the community, 90 (56%) spent no time in the hospital. These subjects make up 12% of the total study sample.

Subjects spent an average of 18 months in the hospital (range 0–107 months) and 12 months on conditional release (range 0–98 months). The system is clearly oriented toward hospitalization, with subjects spending, on average, 68% of their time under PSRB jurisdiction in the hospital, either until the Board discharged them or the study period ended.

The 381 subjects with some time on conditional release had a total of 561 conditional release episodes, an average of 1.5 episodes per subject. Seventy-two percent had 1 episode, 17% had 2 conditional releases, 6% had 3, and 5% had more than 3 conditional releases. During the study period, 56% of those subjects who had some conditional release experienced at least one revocation or voluntary rehospitalization that terminated a conditional release episode. Revocations occurred between 1 and 90 months after conditional release, with a mean of 10 months. Of those subjects revoked by the PSRB, 59% had at least one additional conditional release.

We examined data on 313 conditional release episodes that terminated in revocation or voluntary rehospitalization. Table 4–1 lists the reasons case managers gave for these revocations. Case managers listed multiple reasons for each revocation. It appears that problems that led to revocation developed most frequently in more than one area. Problems between the insanity acquittee and the mental health program included lack of cooperation with treatment, missed appointments, and/or refusal to take medications. These problems also constituted, in most cases, a violation of the conditional release plan and also were listed as such. Another significant reason for revocation was deterioration in the subject's mental condition. Dangerous behavior was listed as a frequent reason for revocation. Most of the reports of dangerousness were associated with clinical deterioration and threats rather than any specific dangerous behavior. These three categories were followed by problems in residential placement, where the primary concern was absence without permission. Case managers reported use of alcohol and drugs in 22% of cases and contacts with the criminal justice system in 15%. Arrests of conditionally released subjects is an important area that is presented in detail in another section of this chapter.

Table 4–1. Reasons for revocation of conditional release (CR)
(N = 313)

Reason	Frequency	Percentage
Problems in mental health services	193	62
Missed appointments	114	36
Uncooperative	60	19
Refused medications	56	18
Violation of CR plan	182	58
Problems with mental condition	180	58
General deterioration	82	26
Agitated, manic, hostile	56	18
Hallucinations, delusions	37	12
Depressed, withdrawn	17	5
Paranoid, suspicious	6	2
Signs of dangerous behavior	156	50
Dangerousness to self or others due to deteriorated mental condition	78	25
Threats and/or assaults on others	74	24
Damage to property	11	4
Suicidal behavior	10	3
Problems in residential functioning	104	33
Use of drugs and/or alcohol	69	22
Contact with criminal justice system	47	15
Problems in interpersonal functioning	40	13
Problems in occupational functioning	28	9
Problems in self- and home maintenance	11	4
Unauthorized driving	9	3
Problems in public deportment	6	2

FACTORS GOVERNING HOSPITALIZATION AND CONDITIONAL RELEASE

To examine variables associated with hospitalization and conditional release, we divided subjects into the same three groups as in our earlier study (1). In forming these groups, we eliminated 72 subjects who were under the Board's jurisdiction for less than 3 months during the study period. These individuals included subjects assigned to the jurisdiction of the Board in the last 3 months of the study period and subjects discharged by the Board at any time during the study period after being under jurisdiction for less than 3 months, including those subjects discharged from the Board's jurisdiction at their first Board hearing. Most of these discharges occurred in the early years of PSRB functioning (see Chapter 5). The three groups consisted of the following:

1. The "not conditionally released" or NCR group, consisting of 320 subjects who spent all of their PSRB time or the entire study period in the hospital.
2. The "conditionally released" or CR group, consisting of 220 subjects initially placed in the hospital by judges and whom the Board later conditionally released at least once during the study period.
3. The "conditionally released by judges" or CRJ group, consisting of 146 subjects whom judges initially placed on conditional release.

We compared these three groups using variables explored in the earlier study of conditional release (1) as well as the expanded data available at this time.

Demographics

The sample consisted of 589 men (86%) and 97 women (14%). Table 4–2 presents gender differences in relation to hospitalization and conditional release. Women were significantly more likely either to be placed on conditional release by Oregon judges or to be conditionally released by the PSRB.

There was a significant difference in the average age of the

Table 4–2. Gender differences in conditional release (*N* = 686)

	Male (*n* = 589)	%	Female (*n* = 97)	%
CRJ: conditional release by judge on assignment to the PSRB	109	18	37	38
CR: conditional release by the PSRB	187	32	33	34
NCR: no conditional release	293	50	27	28

Note. χ^2 = 23.80, df = 2, P = .0000.

three groups, reported at the time of commitment to the jurisdiction of the PSRB (ANOVA, F = 6.405, df = 2,670, P = .0018). The CRJ group had a mean age of 34, compared to 32 for the CR group and 30 for the NCR group. On average, those subjects conditionally released either by judges or by the Board were significantly older than the subjects who spent their entire study time in the hospital.

Diagnosis and Past Contacts With the Mental Health System

There was a significant difference in diagnosis viewed across the three groups (χ^2 = 30.486, df = 12, P = .0024). Judges conditionally released a higher proportion of bipolar disorder subjects and a lower proportion of subjects with schizophrenia, mental retardation, or personality disorders. Schizophrenic subjects whom judges initially assigned to the hospital had an equal chance of being conditionally released by the Board or of spending their entire jurisdictional time hospitalized. Subjects with a diagnosis of mental retardation or of personality disorder were the least likely to be conditionally released by either the judges or the Board.

There was a highly significant difference between the three groups in relation to numbers of past psychiatric hospitalizations (ANOVA, F = 18.068, df = 2,683, P = .0000). The NCR group had, on average, 4.1 prior hospital episodes, compared with 2.7 for the CR and 1.7 for the CRJ groups.

Criminal Justice System Contacts

Table 4–3 presents criminal justice data for the three study groups for the crime leading to PSRB jurisdiction. The proportions of subjects were significantly different across the three groups, with the judges releasing a higher proportion of misdemeanant offenders than were released by the Board. We were interested in the initial decision to hospitalize or conditionally release felony offenders. Although 64% of the CRJ group were assigned to PSRB jurisdiction for felony crimes, these represented the less serious felonies. When we compared the crime seriousness scores for only those subjects with a felony crime, the average score for the CRJ group was 361, significantly less serious than for the other two groups combined, where we found an average score of 339 ($t = 1.98$, df = 514, $P = .0479$).

Once hospitalized, the PSRB conditionally released subjects who were more likely to have been assigned to the jurisdiction of the Board following felony-level crimes. Part of the reason for this lies in the fact that there was a high likelihood that individuals hospitalized following misdemeanor offenses would spend their entire jurisdictional time hospitalized. Of the 540 individuals that the judges assigned to the hospital, the Board conditionally released 45% of the 422 individuals assigned for felony charges compared with only 25% of the 118 individuals assigned for misdemeanor charges ($\chi^2 = 13.342$, df = 1, $P = .0001$).

In contrast to our earlier study (1), we did not find a significant relationship between the seriousness of the crime leading to

Table 4–3.   Crimes leading to PSRB jurisdiction ($N = 686$)

	CRJ ($n = 146$)		CR ($n = 220$)		NCR ($n = 320$)	
Felony crime	94	64%	191	87%	231	72%
Misdemeanor crime[a]	52	36%	29	13%	89	28%
Average seriousness score[b]	429		357		402	

Note.   CRJ = conditional release by judge on assignment to the PSRB; CR = conditional release by the PSRB; NCR = no conditional release.
[a] $\chi^2 = 26.65$, df = 2, $P = .0000$.
[b] ANOVA, $F = 16.99$, df = 2,683, $P = .0000$.

PSRB jurisdiction and the time between hospitalization and conditional release for those subjects with felony crimes. In the earlier study, we found a positive relationship between the seriousness of the crime leading to PSRB jurisdiction and the length of time in hospital prior to conditional release, with those subjects with more serious crimes (or lower scores on the crime seriousness score) spending a longer time in the hospital prior to conditional release.

As presented in Table 4–4, subjects conditionally released by judges had significantly fewer past criminal contacts, both for felonies and for misdemeanors. Those subjects who had no conditional release during the study period had significantly more prior criminal contacts for both felonies and misdemeanors.

Combined Mental Health and Criminal Justice System Contacts

As depicted in Figure 4–1, the judges conditionally released subjects with significantly less prior involvement in both the mental health and criminal justice systems ($\chi^2 = 28.374$, df = 6, $P = .0001$).

Table 4–4.   Prior criminal justice system contacts ($N = 686$)

	CRJ	CR	NCR
Average number of prior criminal justice contacts[a]	2.4	3.8	5.2
Average number of prior criminal contacts per adult year[b]	0.24	0.49	0.60
Average number of prior felony criminal justice contacts[c]	0.84	1.98	2.41
Average number of prior misdemeanor criminal justice contacts[d]	1.53	1.86	2.80

Note. CRJ = conditional release by judge on assignment to the PSRB; CR = conditional release by the PSRB; NCR = no conditional release.
[a] ANOVA, $F = 14.845$, df = 2,683, $P = .0000$.
[b] ANOVA, $F = 6.130$, df = 2,679, $P = .0023$.
[c] ANOVA, $F = 13.306$, df = 2,683, $P = .0000$.
[d] ANOVA, $F = 10.681$, df = 2,683, $P = .0000$.

Revocation

There was no significant difference between the revocation rates for the CRJ group (46%) compared with the CR group (50%). There was also no significant difference between these groups for the time on conditional release before the first revocation took

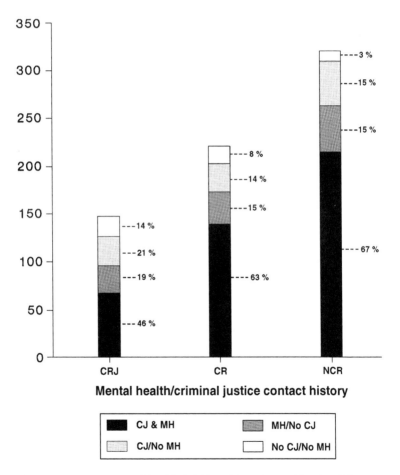

Figure 4–1. Prior mental health (MH) and/or criminal justice (CJ) contacts by conditionally released (CR) status. NCR = not conditionally released; CRJ = conditionally released by judges.

place. However, individuals placed on conditional release by the judges spent only 19% of their total PSRB time or of the study period hospitalized, compared with 50% for the CR group (t = 9.95, df = 364, P = .0000).

Comparison of Those Hospitalized and Conditionally Released by the PSRB

Differences between those whom the Board retained in the hospital and those conditionally released appear to be partially explained by two factors—gender and the crime that led to PSRB jurisdiction. Women were significantly more likely and misdemeanant subjects were significantly less likely to be conditionally released. We explore these two populations in more detail in Chapters 9 and 10.

Comparison of Conditionally Released Subjects With and Without Revocation

We compared the 178 subjects whom the Board revoked from conditional release and the 188 subjects not revoked during the study period. We found that those who were revoked

- Were significantly younger, with an average age of 32 compared with age 34 (t = 2.23, df = 355, P = .0266);
- Were significantly more likely to have a history of substance abuse (i.e., 33% compared to 14%; χ^2 = 18.19, df = 1, P = .0000);
- Were significantly more likely to have a prior hospital episode (i.e., 80% compared with 64%; χ^2 = 11.61, df = 1, P = .0007);
- Had significantly more prior hospital episodes—a mean of 2.8 compared with 1.9 (t = 3.25, df = 364, P = .0013);
- Spent significantly more days in the hospital prior to assignment to PSRB—an average of 468 days compared with 246 (t = 2.48, df = 350, P = .0136);
- Had significantly more contacts with the criminal justice system prior to assignment to PSRB—a mean of 4.5 compared with 2.8 (t = 3.33, df = 364, P = .0010);
- Were significantly more likely to have had a more serious

crime leading to PSRB jurisdiction (i.e., 85% assigned to PSRB for a felony crime compared with 71% of those not revoked assigned to PSRB for a felony crime; χ^2 = 11.38, df = 1, P = .0007);

• Were significantly more likely to have combined prior mental health and criminal justice contacts (i.e., 66% of those revoked had prior contacts in both systems compared with 47% of those who were not revoked; χ^2 = 13.29, df = 1, P = .0003);

• Spent significantly more time while under PSRB jurisdiction in the hospital—an average of 27 months compared with 8 months (t = 10.12, df = 364, P = .0000); and

• Spent a significantly greater amount of their jurisdictional time (or their jurisdictional time to the end of the study period) hospitalized (55% compared with 22%).

Gender, diagnosis, and months on conditional release prior to revocation were not significantly related to revocation.

Criminal Justice Contacts During PSRB Jurisdiction

Subjects were charged with 56 felonies and 49 misdemeanors during the 9-year study period. Table 4–5 lists these criminal contacts presented as felonies and misdemeanors. The table also describes whether the subject was placed in the hospital or in the community on conditional release at the time of the police contact. It is important to note that because of limitations in our data, we only know when the police charged one of the subjects in the study. We are not certain that the alleged crime took place while the individual was in the placement in which he or she was charged. For example, it is possible that a crime may have been committed while a person was on conditional release and charges filed when the person was in the hospital. Given this caveat, police reported 73% of the felony and 88% of the misdemeanor contacts at the time subjects were on conditional release.

The most frequent felony contacts were in the group of burglary, robbery, and theft, accounting for 21% of the reported crimes. The most frequently occurring misdemeanor contacts were for theft (17% of the charges), followed by driving under the

Table 4–5. Criminal justice contacts during PSRB ($N = 686$)

Crime category	Total contacts Frequency	%	Release contacts Frequency	%	Hospital contacts Frequency	%
Felony crimes	56	53	41	49	15	71
Burglary/ robbery/theft	22	21	16	19	6	29
Assault	6	6	5	6	1	5
Drug offenses	5	5	2	2	3	14
Unauthorized use of motor vehicle	4	4	2	2	2	10
Eluding police officer	4	4	4	5		
Failure to appear	3	3	3	4		
Homicide	2	2	2	2		
Felony driving while license suspended	2	2	2	2		
Rape	2	2	1	1	1	5
Sex abuse	2	2	1	1	1	5
Criminal mischief	1	1	1	1		
Intimidation	1	1	1	1		
Perjury	1	1	1	1		
Arson	1	1	1	1		
Misdemeanor crimes	49	47	43	51	6	29
Theft	18	17	14	17	4	19
Driving under the influence	11	10	11	13		
Assault	7	7	6	7	1	5
Menacing/ harassment	3	3	3	4		
Driving offenses	3	3	2	2	1	5
Criminal mischief	2	2	2	2		
Trespass	1	1	1	1		
Public indecency	1	1	1	1		
Reckless endangerment	1	1	1	1		
Failure to pay fine	1	1	1	1		
Resisting arrest	1	1	1	1		
Escape/fugitive			21		46	
Escape/fugitive from other agency	67					

influence (10%). Of the serious felonies against persons, there was one rape involving a hospitalized subject. There were only a small number of criminal contacts for hospitalized subjects, including one reported rape and six assaults. Conditionally released subjects were charged with two homicides, three assaults, and one incident of arson.

Overall, 15% of conditionally released subjects had contacts with the police while they were on conditional release. There were 41 felony and 43 misdemeanor arrests for these subjects. This amounts to an average of 0.23 contacts per released subject, with a rate of 0.12 criminal justice contacts per year of conditional release time. (To put these figures into perspective, the 366 subjects with conditional release spent a total of 8,321 months or 694 years on conditional release.)

Contacts related to escape are listed separately on the table, because it was not clear from our data which escapes were actually crimes and which were notations on the police computer reflecting a notice to the police that the Board had revoked a subject. Regardless of whether they were actual charged crimes or were notations, these were primarily related to hospitalized subjects. Forty-six of these escapes (69%) took place while a subject was hospitalized. We do not know if each subject actually walked away from the hospital or was on pass when the "escape" took place.

DISCUSSION

In this chapter, we describe the functioning of the PSRB in relation to the critical areas of hospitalization, conditional release, and revocation. One characteristic of this system that was immediately apparent was its heavy reliance on the forensic hospital. We have demonstrated, in this and in other chapters in this book, that although Oregon has been one of the pioneering states in relation to the conditional release of insanity acquittees, the Oregon system favors inpatient treatment. Both the Oregon judges and the Board appear to use conditional release in a conservative manner. The sample of 758 individuals spent, on average, 68% of their PSRB jurisdiction or of the study period, hospitalized. Further, those subjects the trial court judges did not place on conditional release had only a 50% chance of experiencing any conditional release. On the other end of the spectrum, 12% of the sample the judges placed on conditional release were never hospitalized.

The decision by the judges to place 146 individuals on conditional release appears to represent (as we would expect) relatively conservative decision making. The judges typically conditionally released older subjects who had psychiatric diagnoses such as bipolar disorder that are more likely to come under control quickly. In addition, these released subjects had fewer past mental health and criminal justice contacts. They had less serious crimes leading to PSRB jurisdiction and had significantly fewer past criminal justice contacts, including significantly fewer felony and misdemeanor contacts.

Although we did not study this area, it is interesting to speculate on the nature of the data available to the trial court judge at the time he or she made a decision to place a subject on conditional release. Typically at sentencing, judges would have information about the index crime that led to the insanity hearing and information on past arrests and convictions. They would also know something about the subject's past psychiatric history as presented in the reports of the psychiatrist or psychologist who evaluated the subject for the insanity defense. However, they would not have all the information gathered by this research project regarding past contact with the mental health system and, to some extent, with the criminal justice system. Although we have concerns about the quality of the information available to judges (2), it appears from our current data that they had enough information to make rulings in a consistent manner.

Women and misdemeanant subjects clearly have unique careers in this system, and these careers form the basis of separate chapters in this book (Chapters 9 and 10). Women were more likely to be conditionally released either by the judges or the Board. Surprisingly, misdemeanants who were not initially placed on conditional release by judges were more likely, compared with felons, to spend their entire jurisdictional time in the forensic hospital. This finding raises questions about whether the PSRB system currently operates in a fair manner for those misdemeanants who are hospitalized. This area is explored in more detail in Chapter 9.

If women and misdemeanant subjects are removed from consideration, there were few clues in our data base to help distinguish male felons who were continuously hospitalized from those who did get to experience conditional release and monitored community care. The finding from our earlier study that those with more serious crimes leading to PSRB jurisdiction had longer hospitalizations prior to being placed on conditional release was not confirmed in this larger study. However, the subjects' diagnoses and the severity of their condition may provide some clues for further exploration. We did find a significant correlation between diagnosis and conditional release, which is discussed further in Chapter 8. Those subjects who spent their entire jurisdictional time or the entire study period hospitalized had the highest mean number of past psychiatric hospitalizations. They also had significantly more past felonies and misdemeanors. Because subjects whom the Board conditionally released also had extensive past experience with the criminal justice system, we can speculate here that the decision to conditionally release may have been more closely related to the subject's diagnosis and mental status during hospitalization, rather than to past criminal justice contacts or to the crime that led to PSRB jurisdiction.

This is an important area that we intend to pursue in future research projects. It is critical to know how conditional release decisions are made and what factors enter into decision making in individual cases. It is also important to know if decisions regarding conditional release were related more to current mental functioning than to past criminal activities. If this were found to be true, it would suggest that, by focusing release decisions on current symptom expression of mental illness rather than on past criminal justice history, the system has functioned in a manner appropriate to its obligations to insanity acquittees and to society.

As we discuss in detail in Chapter 12, if an insanity defense were to be a meaningful and fair method of dealing with mentally ill insanity acquittees, the system should operate with a primary focus on mental functioning of the insanity acquittee. In addition, there is an additional heavy reliance in the Oregon system on hospitalization. This reflects the other prong of the insanity sentence—the protection of society. Whether this reliance on the forensic hospital is too conservative awaits further empirical investigation, especially (as we discuss in this chapter and again in Chapter 12) with the development of the provision for conditional release and monitored community treatment. Revocation is another critical variable related to the functioning of this system. In a previous article (3), we found a revocation rate of 51% for those placed on conditional release in one large treatment program during the first 3 years of operation of the PSRB. We speculated about whether this revocation rate reflected an accurate assessment of the patient's needs or was inordinately influenced by the public safety goals of the PSRB system. The most frequent reasons given in this earlier study for revocation were deteriorating mental status, coupled with noncompliance with supervision and treatment.

With statewide data and a 9-year sample, we have a nearly identical revocation rate of 49% of those individuals placed on conditional release. We also found similar reasons for revocation in this study, including noncooperation with the treatment program, deterioration of mental status, violations of the conditional release plan, and behaviors that were considered by the programs to be dangerous. This latter group appears to contain more concerns about dangerousness than actual dangerous behavior. In addition, as one might expect, we found that problems in residential placement and the use of alcohol and drugs while on conditional release were important reasons for revocation.

We also have additional information about revocation from the comparison of those subjects whom the Board revoked and those not revoked from their conditional release. The revoked subjects were younger, had a prior history of more substance abuse, had more prior contacts with both the mental health and criminal justice systems, and had more serious crimes leading to PSRB jurisdiction. Once under PSRB jurisdiction, they spent more time in the hospital prior to conditional release and a greater percentage of time overall in the hospital during the study period. Once conditionally released, diagnosis and gender were not significantly associated with revocation.

These findings clearly point to a group of individuals with difficult problems expressed in terms of prior criminality, frequency of past psychiatric hospitalization, and increased substance abuse. It would not be surprising that individuals who share these characteristics would spend more time in a hospital prior to conditional release and would have a harder time adjusting once they are back in the community, especially in a system that is keyed to attempt to prevent behaviors that are dangerous to others.

However, we are left with many unanswered questions about revocation. From a national point of view, there are now some studies that contribute information about revocation. An earlier study from Maryland (4) demonstrated a revocation rate of 41% of the insanity acquittees. A more recent study from the same jurisdiction reported a much higher revocation rate of 64% for subjects conditionally released from the forensic hospital and 79% of insanity acquittees conditionally released from civil hospitalization (5). Rogers and Cavanaugh (6), working with a highly selected population in Illinois, reported a revocation rate of 25%. Two studies focused on the conditional release of insanity acquittees in California; one study reported a revocation rate of 48% (7), whereas another reported a rate of 21% (8). Another study from New York demonstrated a revocation rate of only 5% (9). In this latter study, the authors explained the discrepancy between their finding and the other findings reported in the literature, based on the fact that a conditionally released insanity acquittee in New York can only be revoked at a court hearing where revocation is based on evidence of dangerousness. Given the reasons for revocation listed above for our sample, if the New York standards were applied in Oregon and if a court hearing were required, we would expect a much lower revocation rate.

These studies raise more questions than they answer. The wide range of revocation rates no doubt reflects differences in how conditional release is managed in these different jurisdictions. These differences would include how closely an acquittee is monitored while on conditional release and how easily an acquittee can be revoked. This is an area that needs further empirical study, as a component of a research agenda focused on conditional release.

New crimes committed by insanity acquittees are important to any system designed for monitoring insanity acquittees. As described in Chapter 1, the PSRB was established in Oregon following widespread dissatisfaction with the preexisting system, mainly because of the view that the system did not sufficiently protect the public from insanity acquittees. This concern was particularly focused on those individuals who had been discharged from the forensic hospital and came to public attention by committing new offenses. The current system for release from the forensic hospital is based on a tightly designed conditional release program that follows statutory direction to protect the public. This is the core feature of the Oregon system. One significant measure of its success will be crimes committed by conditionally released subjects. The data presented in this chapter are encouraging in this area. There were several serious offenses; however, overall there were relatively few criminal justice contacts involving PSRB subjects. With the exception of the escapes, there were 105 criminal contacts, 21 (20%) reported for inpatients and 84 (80%) for conditionally released outpatients.

Given the balancing of interests that are necessarily at the core of this system, do the criminal justice contacts reported for PSRB subjects on conditional release (as depicted in Table 4–5) represent an acceptable record? We would assume that the answer to this question will depend on who examines Table 4–5 and what their biases might be. Researchers, politicians, jurists, legal theorists, and victims will view these data differently. At this point, there are only a few empirical studies that can help put the Oregon figures in a national perspective. As reported in this chapter, 15% of subjects with conditional release were rearrested while on conditional release. This is closer to the rearrest rate of 6% presented in the California study (8) than to the rate of 47% and 63% reported for the two groups in the Maryland study (5). This is another important area awaiting further research.

The conventional method of approaching the question of society's tolerance of crime and the costs of such crime is found in the division of crimes into those against persons, those against property, and those without victims (victimless crimes). The leading group of crimes charged against subjects on conditional release were burglary, robbery, and/or theft, accounting for 19%

of the felonies and 17% of the misdemeanor crimes. In addition, there were nine serious felony crimes against persons: five assaults, two homicides, one rape, and one case of sexual abuse. In one homicide, the subject killed his mother a week after he had walked away from his community placement. The second homicide involved a vehicular accident, caused by the reckless driving of a manic subject, in which two persons were killed. Both cases resulted in civil suits. In the first case, the community program was not held liable to a charge of negligent supervision. However, this case did raise significant concerns about potential liability related to the community supervision of insanity acquittees. As a result of this case, the Division developed a method to provide liability protection for conditionally released insanity acquittees (see Chapter 1). In the civil suit related to the vehicular homicide case, the Oregon Court of Appeals and the Oregon Supreme Court upheld the statutory primacy of protection of the public as the major function of the PSRB, although it left the question of whether the community program owed a duty to the driving public to the trial court (10). Following these appeals, the community program settled with the plaintiff, and this particular question remained unresolved. The number of very serious crimes needs to be balanced against the fact that subjects in this study spent a total of 694 years on conditional release.

Escape also represents an extremely important issue in relation to forensic patients, especially inpatients. There should be a relationship between the nature of the security system at a forensic hospital and the number of escapes from the particular facility. Problems created by escapes were graphically illustrated in Oregon in the spring of 1991, when an insanity acquittee escaped from the forensic hospital while on a chaperoned pass. Although the police apprehended him without incident about 3 weeks later, this was a highly controversial escape, because the individual had been committed a decade earlier to the jurisdiction of the PSRB following a double homicide.

Even though there were no major negative consequences related to this escape, it produced a great outcry in the media and was widely discussed in the Oregon legislature, which was in session when these events took place. The debate, both in the press and in the legislature, was highly inflammatory. There was a precipitous rush to label all forensic patients as being extremely dangerous, and much criticism leveled at the hospital and its security procedures. There were proposals made to transfer the forensic hospital to the Corrections Division and suggestions to move the forensic facility away from the state capital to rural Oregon. Forensic patients were also portrayed in an extremely negative light. The debate never focused on the fact that there needs to be a balance between a forensic hospital that is constructed as a fortress and one that functions as a sieve. Nor did the debate address the issue that the security system in any particular jurisdiction should be designed only after careful reflection about the needs of mentally ill insanity acquittees and of the greater population.

Conditionally released subjects also escape. It is difficult to get an accurate picture of the actual number of such incidents for the subjects in our sample. Some are reflected in revocations—some subjects may actually have been charged with a crime, and others may have had a revocation noted in the police computer. These events represent the failure of agreements between the insanity acquittee and the community program and are potentially serious problems. Although we do not have this information directly, we postulate that a percentage of the crimes listed in Table 4–5 involved conditionally released subjects while they were on escape status. Unsupervised insanity acquittees on escape status are just what this system was designed to prevent. This is another area in which further investigation is necessary. It is important to know what the consequences of escape are for those who leave the hospital and those who walk away from community programs.

In this chapter, we have examined the critical areas of hospitalization, conditional release, and revocation of insanity acquittees in the Oregon system. In Chapter 1, we distinguished the roles and responsibilities of the Board and of the Division. The Board's specific role governs placement of insanity acquittees in the hospital or in the community and movement from one to the other site. This chapter and Chapter 5 are the primary chapters in this book that examine how the Board functions with regard to these placement decisions. Here we described these functions by examining subject characteristics. In the next chapter, we look at trends in determining how the Board functioned over a 12-year time period.

REFERENCES

1. Bloom JD, Rogers JL, Manson SM: After Oregon's insanity defense: a comparison of conditional release and hospitalization. Int J Law Psychiatry 5:391–402, 1982
2. Reichlin SM, Bloom JD, Williams MH: Excluding personality disorders from the insanity defense—a follow-up study. Unpublished study, 1991
3. Bloom JD, Williams MH, Rogers JL, et al: Evaluation and treatment of insanity acquittees in the community. Bull Am Acad Psychiatry Law 14:231–244, 1986
4. Goldmeier J, White EV, Ulrich C, et al: Community intervention with the mentally ill offender: a residential program. Bull Am Acad Psychiatry Law 8:72–81, 1980
5. Tellefsen C, Cohen MI, Silver SB, et al: Predicting success on conditional release for insanity acquittees: regionalized versus non-regionalized hospital patients. Bull Am Acad Psychiatry Law 20:87–100, 1992
6. Rogers R, Cavanaugh JL: A program for potentially violent offender patients. International Journal of Offender Therapy and Comparative Criminology 25:53–59, 1981
7. Lamb HR, Weinberger LE, Gross BH: Court-mandated community outpatient treatment for persons found Not Guilty by Reason of Insanity: a five-year follow-up. Am J Psychiatry 145:450–456, 1988
8. Wiederanders MR: Recidivism of disordered offenders who were conditionally vs. unconditionally released. Behavioral Sciences and the Law 10:141–148, 1992
9. McGreevy MA, Steadman HJ, Dvoskin JA, et al: New York State's system of managing insanity acquittees in the community. Hosp Community Psychiatry 42:512–517, 1991
10. Cain v Rijken, 74 Or. App. 76, 700 P.2d 1061 (1985); Cain v Rijken, 300 Or. 706, 717 P.2d 140 (1986)

Chapter 5

Trends in Hospital Utilization by Insanity Acquittees

In this chapter, we examine the effect of the Psychiatric Security Review Board (PSRB) on the census of the Oregon State Hospital forensic unit. Although the number of insanity acquittals in the United States each year is smaller than often assumed by both the general public and professionals (1, 2), this population utilizes a significant amount of mental health resources. In a 1978 national survey of admissions to facilities for offenders with mental disorders, 8% were insanity acquittees. However, on an average day, this group made up more than 22% of the resident population (3). These figures reflect the unusually long hospitalizations of this population. One study of insanity acquittees admitted to state hospitals in New York from 1971 to 1976 found that the average length of hospitalization was 3.5 years (4).

A recent paper (5) surveyed state mental health forensic program directors and found that on a single day in 1986, there were 5,424 hospitalized insanity acquittees in the United States. Of these, 3,735 were in forensic hospital units and 1,689 were hospitalized in civil facilities. There was great variation in the numbers of such patients by state when the number of insanity acquittees was corrected for varying state populations. Expressed in rates per 100,000 persons, Oregon was near the top of the list, with a rate of 10.04, only slightly behind the rate of 10.92 for Hawaii, and well behind the leading jurisdiction, the District of Columbia, with a rate of 61.66 hospitalized insanity acquittees per 100,000.

Additionally, there are data suggesting that the number of insanity acquittees has been increasing over the past 20 years. In

The authors wish to thank Douglas Bigelow, Ph.D., Bentson McFarland, M.D., Ph.D., and James Carlson for their work on an earlier version of this chapter.

Oregon, as depicted in Figure 5–1, the average daily inpatient forensic population of persons found not guilty by reason of insanity (NGRI) climbed dramatically during the early 1970s. This population climbed from 30 at the beginning of 1974 to a high of 163 in 1980. This expansion of the inpatient forensic population in Oregon coincided with the introduction of the

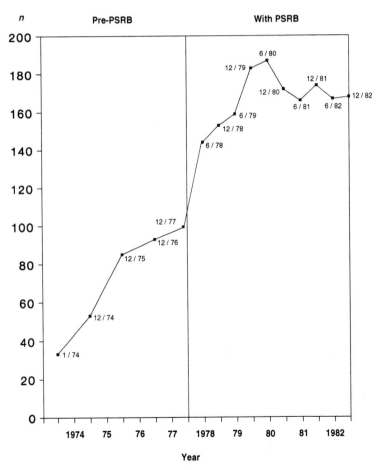

Figure 5–1. Forensic patients in Oregon State Hospital following insanity defense (1974–1982).

American Law Institute test for insanity in 1970 and with the introduction of the PSRB in 1978 (6).

As we described in Chapter 1, the insanity sentence is served in either the forensic hospital or in the community on conditional release. The PSRB controls movement between the hospital and the community, and it therefore controls entry and exit from the forensic hospital. Once a trial court assigns an individual to the jurisdiction of the PSRB and specifies the initial placement either in the hospital or on conditional release, the Board may exercise four options that control the movement of the individual between the hospital and the community. The Board can order the individual to be 1) hospitalized, 2) conditionally released into the community, 3) revoked from a conditional release and returned to the hospital, or 4) discharged from PSRB jurisdiction.

Figure 5–2 shows how each of these four options affects the inpatient forensic census. There are two ways for an insanity acquittee to enter the hospital—either on assignment from the trial court or following a revocation of conditional release. Likewise, there are two ways for an individual to leave the hospital— either by having been placed on conditional release by the Board or following a discharge from the jurisdiction of the Board. Each of the four components of Figure 5–2 is examined in this chapter.

Figure 5–3 continues the depiction begun in Figure 5–1 and shows the state hospital forensic census from the inception of the PSRB system in 1978 through 1989. Of particular interest is the

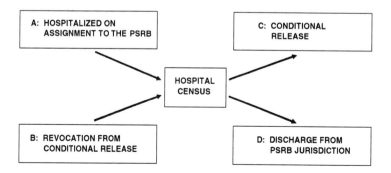

Figure 5–2. Board actions affecting hospital census.

sharp rise in inpatient population that began in 1984 and continued through 1988. For both economic and public policy reasons, it is important to understand the factors that influence hospital census, especially with this steep rise in inpatient census, because the costs of providing hospital services to the forensic population are considerable (7) (see Chapter 11).

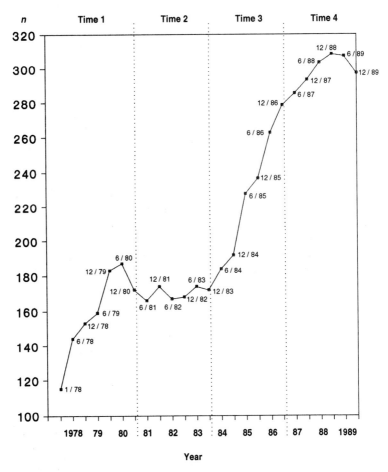

Figure 5–3. PSRB clients in Oregon State Hospital based on monthly census (1978–1989).

The Oregon Mental Health and Developmental Disabilities Services Division (the Division) provides both hospital and community services for PSRB clients. Given the sharp rise in inpatient census, the Division was required to open new wards to meet the demands of the increased PSRB population. This rise in the inpatient census peaked in 1988, but the vulnerability of the entire system to fluctuations in the PSRB census was clearly demonstrated. Because of the possible reciprocal effects of changes in the forensic census on the mental health system as a whole, it is important to explore the dynamics of hospital population fluctuations. This chapter deals with the time period depicted in Figure 5–3—1978–1989—and explores the hospital census during this time period in light of the four factors illustrated in Figure 5–2, two of which lead to a census increase and two to a hospital census decrease.

Data for this chapter derive from the PSRB Research Data Base (see Chapter 3), in which we document the movement of all individuals under the jurisdiction of the Board and that we update yearly. Because of the availability of data on subject movements through 1989, and because of changes we have noted in such movements during the period 1987–1989, we have expanded the time period in this chapter beyond the period covered in the remainder of the book. In addition, because we are concerned in this chapter with movements of all PSRB clients as they affect the hospital census, we have included those individuals who successfully raised an insanity defense prior to 1978 and whom the trial courts assigned to the jurisdiction of the PSRB when it began operation in 1978. For the same reasons, we have included as separate entries the multiple episodes of assignment to PSRB jurisdiction. Thus from 1978 through 1989, trial court judges assigned 1,156 cases to the Board's jurisdiction. Of these, 1,013 (88%) spent some time in the hospital. These 1,013 PSRB clients compose the sample for this chapter.

Figure 5–3 shows the PSRB hospital population for 1978–1989, based on monthly population census. The figure lends itself to division into four distinct time periods, each of 3 years duration. The first 3-year interval, Time 1, reflects the initial population rise following the introduction of the PSRB. Time 2 shows a period of stabilization, and Time 3 shows a dramatic increase in the population, which peaked in Time 4. As discussed previously, at the time PSRB began operation, the trial court assigned 152 individuals found NGRI prior to 1978 to the jurisdiction of the Board. In Figure 5–3, the starting hospital census includes 112 of these "pre-PSRB" individuals who were in the hospital when the PSRB began operation on January 1, 1978.

We examined a number of factors that might contribute to an understanding of the differences in these four time periods, with a special focus on the sharp rise in hospital census in Time 3. We examined demographic characteristics of hospitalized PSRB clients to see if there were differences in patient characteristics across the four time periods that might account for the changes in the hospital census. We considered the possibility that the increase in Time 3 might have been because of an increasing number of patients in the hospital with long jurisdictions and lengthy hospital stays. Finally, we examined each of the four areas depicted in Figure 5–2 to determine the comparative contribution of each area to changes in the PSRB hospital census.

PATIENT CHARACTERISTICS

To explore changes in the patient population and its effects on census, we constructed demographic profiles for the PSRB cohorts. We divided the sample into five cohorts (Table 5–1) and compared the groups in terms of gender, age on assignment to PSRB, and diagnosis. The first cohort consists of those individuals found NGRI prior to 1978 and assigned to PSRB jurisdiction for management. The remaining four cohorts consist of 3-year entry cohorts based on year of assignment to PSRB jurisdiction.

There was a significant difference among the five cohorts in the ratio of male and female hospitalized PSRB clients. However, when we excluded the "pre-78" cohort, there was no significant difference among the remaining four cohorts. Subjects ranged in age from 17 to 83, with a mean varying from 29 to a high of 34 in the Time 4 cohort. A Newman-Keuls post-hoc comparison between groups showed that the "pre-78" cohort was significantly younger than the remaining cohorts and accounted for the significant difference in age.

Table 5-1. PSRB admission profiles

	Pre-1978 n	%	1978–1980 n	%	1981–1983 n	%	1984–1986 n	%	1987–1989 n	%	Total n	%
n	122		279		225		225		162		1,013	
Gender[a]												
Male	117	96	251	90	194	86	197	88	136	84	895	88
Female	5	4	28	10	31	14	28	12	26	16	118	12
Age[b]	29		31		32		31		34		31	
Diagnosis[c]												
Psychotic	86	75	179	71	159	76	128	72	67	73	619	73
Personality disorder	11	10	46	18	24	11	22	12	14	15	117	14
Mentally deficient	5	4	16	6	20	10	18	10	8	9	67	8
OBS	13	11	10	4	6	3	11	6	3	3	43	5
Crime leading to PSRB[d]												
Felony	110	90	212	76	167	74	165	73	138	85	792	78
Misdemeanor	12	10	67	24	58	26	60	27	24	15	221	22
Length of PSRB jurisdiction[e]												
1 year	12	10	61	22	56	25	52	23	23	14	204	20
5 years	27	22	91	33	71	32	66	29	40	25	295	29
10 years	20	16	37	13	34	15	41	18	28	17	160	16
20 years	45	37	69	25	55	24	46	20	52	32	267	26
> 20 years	18	15	21	7	9	4	20	9	18	11	86	9

[a] $\chi^2 = 11.641$, df = 4, $P = .0202$; [b] $F = 3.763$, df = 4,994, $P = .0048$; [c] $\chi^2 = 23.712$, df = 12, $P = .0222$; [d] $\chi^2 = 43.627$, df = 4, $P = .0003$; [e] $\chi^2 = 43.627$, df = 16, $P = .0002$.

Overall, we found a marginal difference in the five cohorts for diagnostic categories. The "pre-78" cohort had a larger proportion of subjects with organic brain disorder and relatively smaller proportion of subjects with personality disorder or mentally deficient diagnosis. With the "pre-78" cohort excluded, there was no significant difference among the remaining four cohorts. Thus, if we exclude the "pre-PSRB" group, the subjects were similar in gender, age, and diagnosis in each of the four time periods.

We compared the type of crime leading to PSRB jurisdiction, reflected in Table 5–1 in the misdemeanor/felony ratio and in the length of assignment to PSRB jurisdiction, and found significant differences between the five cohorts. Even with the "pre-78" cohort excluded, we found a significant difference between the remaining four cohorts for both types of crime ($\chi^2 = 8.75$, df = 3, $P = .0328$) and length of assignment to PSRB ($\chi^2 = 22.29$, df = 12, $P = .0344$). With both the "pre-78" and the Time 4 cohorts excluded, there were no significant differences between the three cohorts in Times 1–3 on these two variables. The "pre-78" and the Time 4 groups resemble each other in the increased percentage of felony crimes and decreased percentage of misdemeanor crimes leading to assignment to the PSRB.

THE BUILDUP OF LONG-TERM PATIENTS

We next considered whether the dramatic rise in hospital census in Time 3 could be partially accounted for by a buildup of patients with lengthy jurisdictions and long hospital stays. If the increased hospital census was due to more seriously ill or dangerous individuals remaining in the hospital, one would expect to see an increase over time in the proportion of hospitalized patients with longer periods of PSRB jurisdiction.

Individuals are assigned to the PSRB for the maximum period of time allowed in sentencing had they been convicted of the offense with which they were charged. Typically, these jurisdiction periods fall into one of five categories: 1 year or less for misdemeanor offenses; 5 years; 10 years; 20 years; and more than 20 years, including life sentences for felony offenses. Table 5–2 presents the proportion of subjects from these five jurisdiction categories in the hospital at some time during each of six 2-year intervals. Some differences can be seen, such as the higher percentage of subjects in the "> 20-year" group in the latest time periods and the lower percentage of subjects in the "1-year" group. However, these differences were not significant. And if we focus on the period of increased population in the hospital census from 1984 to 1988, it does not appear to be a result of a buildup of chronic patients with lengthy jurisdictional periods, because the proportion assigned for 20 years or more remained fairly stable during that period and increased following that period. We found similar results when we looked at 1-year intervals instead of the 2-year intervals presented in Table 5–2.

Although we could not account for the fluctuations in hospital census based on a buildup of long-term subjects, we considered the possibility that certain entry cohorts contributed disproportionately to a buildup of subjects in the hospital. Table 5–3 shows the percentage of six 2-year entry cohorts in the hospital during subsequent 2-year periods. Comparing the percentage remaining in the hospital 2 years after assignment to the PSRB shows that the later entry cohorts were less likely to be released from the hospital. For example, 63% of the subjects assigned to the PSRB in 1980–1981 were in the hospital in 1982–1983, compared with 88% of the subjects assigned to the PSRB in 1986–1987 who were in the hospital during the following 2 years. However, in addition to changes in the release rates for the later cohorts, it appears that, overall, the system changed for all cohorts after 1983. In addition to the 2-year comparisons shown in Table 5–3, we also compared 1-year entry cohorts and examined each subsequent year of hospitalization under the PSRB. For the 1981 and 1982 assignment cohorts, there were increases in the hospitalization rates subsequent to the year 1983, indicating that more subjects were revoked from conditional release than the number discharged or placed on conditional release.

BOARD ACTIONS AFFECTING HOSPITAL CENSUS

As shown in Figure 5–2, there are two actions in this system that lead to an increase in hospital census and two actions that lead to

Table 5–2. Length of PSRB jurisdiction (number of hospital census cohort in each jurisdiction range)

	1978–1979		1980–1981		1982–1983		1984–1985		1986–1987		1988–1989		Total	
	n	%	n	%	n	%	n	%	n	%	n	%	n	%
1 year	45	15	58	16	51	15	47	13	39	10	25	6	204	20
5 years	96	31	106	29	95	28	95	26	109	27	97	23	295	29
10 years	42	14	52	14	61	18	74	21	79	19	85	20	160	16
20 years	96	31	114	31	106	31	109	30	132	32	156	37	267	26
> 20 years	30	10	35	10	29	8	34	9	48	12	63	15	86	9

Table 5–3. PSRB admission cohorts and subsequent hospitalization (number hospitalized during each time period)

Assignment year	1978–1979		1980–1981		1982–1983		1984–1985		1986–1987		1988–1989		Total
	n	%	n	%	n	%	n	%	n	%	n	%	
1978–1979	307		210	68	115	37	69	22	60	20	51	17	322
1980–1981			155		97	63	53	34	38	25	32	21	163
1982–1983					129		90	70	67	52	45	35	141
1984–1985							145		111	77	87	60	150
1986–1987									132		116	88	141
1988–1989											96		96

a decrease in hospital census. Figure 5–4 depicts the two actions that lead to an increase in hospital census: the number of subjects trial courts placed in the hospital at the time of the initial assignment to PSRB jurisdiction and the Board-ordered revocations from conditional release. Figure 5–5 shows the two actions that lead to a decrease in hospital census: conditional release from the hospital and discharge from PSRB jurisdiction for hospitalized subjects.

In Figure 5–4, graph A, the number of subjects the trial courts initially placed in the hospital at the time of assignment to PSRB jurisdiction was at its highest during the first 2 years of the Board's existence, then decreased to a relatively constant rate of assignments during Time 2 and Time 3, and began to decrease again in Time 4. The decrease in Time 4 reflects the decrease in the number of successful insanity defenses in the courts, most likely related to a decrease in the number of individuals raising the insanity defense. The decrease is not the result of trial courts placing more individuals on conditional release. The initial increase in the hospital census during Time 1 might be related to the court hospital assignments during that period. However, this factor by itself does not appear to explain the sharp increase in forensic hospital census during Time 3, because the rate of initial assignments to the hospital remained relatively stable during that period.

Graph B in Figure 5–4 demonstrates that the number of revocations was low during Time 1, increased to a relatively stable rate during Time 2 and Time 3, and began to decrease during the end of Time 4. Again, this factor may explain some of the initial increase in the hospital census during Time 1 but does not appear to account for the increase during Time 3. Similarly, the decrease in the number of revocations at the end of Time 4 may account in part for the corresponding decrease in hospital census during that period.

The two graphs in Figure 5–5 demonstrate that the rates of conditional releases and discharges were higher during Time 2 than during Time 1 or Time 3 and dropped substantially during Time 4. Graph B in Figure 5–5 shows the changes in mandatory and discretionary discharges as well as the total number of discharges. The pattern of mandatory discharges remained fairly

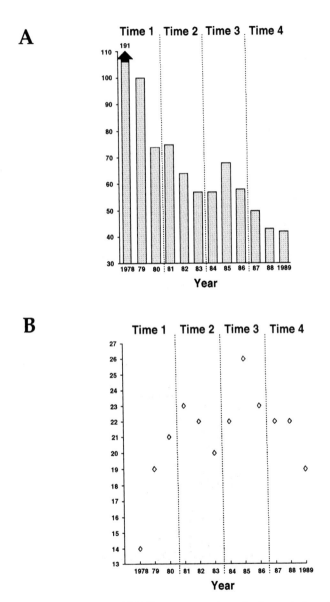

Figure 5–4. Rates of PSRB movement into the forensic hospital.
A: hospitalized on assignment to PSRB; *B:* percentage revoked from
conditional release.

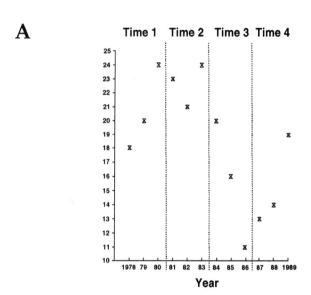

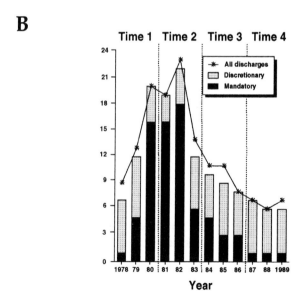

Figure 5–5. Rates of PSRB movement out of the forensic hospital.
A: percentage placed on conditional release from hospital;
B: percentage in hospital discharged from PSRB jurisdiction.

constant over the 12 years, averaging 6% of the yearly hospital census. The greatest differences over the years occurred in the discretionary discharge category. The number of subjects the Board discharged as no longer mentally ill or no longer dangerous varied greatly from 1% of the hospital census in 1978 to a high of 13% in 1982. By the end of Time 4, the Board was discharging fewer than 1% of the hospital census in this manner.

To determine whether or not the variation in these four factors was statistically significant, we computed chi-squared tests comparing the expected rates during 6-month periods with the observed rates. Expected rates were computed under the hypothesis of constant rates and were adjusted for variations in the hospital population or conditional release population. Table 5–4 shows the chi-squared values for the four time periods and the overall 12-year study period. Overall, the observed rate of discretionary discharges deviated most strongly from the expected rate. Although the rate for initial court assignment to the hospital was also significantly different from the expected rate overall, when Time 1 figures were eliminated, there was no longer a significant result. This outcome is probably because of the higher numbers of subjects successfully raising an insanity defense during 1978–1979. Similarly, we found a significant difference between the observed and expected rates of revocation during Time 1, which was most likely due to the smaller numbers of subjects on conditional release at that time. Overall, within the four time periods, the rates of the four factors were roughly homogeneous except for discretionary discharges.

DISCUSSION

We found few changes of any significance in either the demographic or criminal justice variables of the hospitalized insanity acquittees during the study period. Consistent with earlier studies of this population, we found that those individuals found NGRI prior to the beginning of the PSRB and assigned to its jurisdiction in 1978 (the "pre-78" cohort) differed in significant respects from individuals raising successful insanity defenses after the PSRB began operating. The subjects in the "pre-78" group were more likely to be male, were younger, had more organic diagnoses (although they were still predominantly psychotic), and raised the insanity defense against more serious criminal charges. The most interesting finding in terms of criminal justice variables is that the subjects in Time 4 are similar to the "pre-78" cohort in terms of the seriousness of the crime leading to PSRB jurisdiction. This is true even though the Time 4 cohort has an increased proportion of females who traditionally are assigned to the PSRB for less serious offenses.

The findings in this chapter show that there is a chronic segment of the hospitalized population that clearly contributes to

Table 5–4.   Chi-square values for PSRB movements

	Time 1 (df = 5)	Time 2 (df = 5)	Time 3 (df = 5)	Time 4 (df = 5)	Total (df = 23)
Court assigned to hospital					
χ^2	12.90	2.28	2.82	4.97	43.01
P	.0243	NS	NS	NS	.0069
Revocation					
χ^2	13.02	4.11	5.95	4.81	30.81
P	.0211	NS	NS	NS	NS
Conditional release					
χ^2	3.98	4.21	10.33	9.60	61.46
P	NS	NS	NS	NS	.0000
Discharge from the PSRB					
χ^2	13.52	26.32	3.35	3.90	149.56
P	.0189	.0001	NS	NS	.0000
Mandatory discharges					
χ^2	9.56	5.80	4.41	3.27	25.24
P	NS	NS	NS	NS	NS
Discretionary discharges					
χ^2	41.73	31.16	6.39	2.18	290.05
P	.0000	.0000	NS	NS	.0000

the hospital census. Of the 422 clients who were under PSRB jurisdiction for more than 4 years during this 12-year study period, 123 (29%) spent their entire PSRB period in the hospital. However, a buildup of these long-term hospitalized subjects does not account for the sharp rise in the census from 1984 to 1988. Instead, there appears to be an increase in hospitalized patients regardless of the length of PSRB jurisdiction ranges that affected all entry cohorts from 1983 through 1989.

We next turn to the four areas depicted in Figure 5–2. This figure depicts a very complex set of decisions made at multiple levels in the system. For example, changes within the state mental health system may mean that fewer individuals are considered for release from the hospital. Although a periodic review of PSRB cases is mandated by the legislature, considerations for conditional release or discretionary discharge often are initiated by hospital staff when they think that the individual has improved sufficiently to warrant such release from the hospital. Therefore, problems that existed elsewhere in the system during Time 3, such as staffing shortages in the hospital or a saturation of community placements available for conditionally released PSRB clients, may have an impact on the functioning of the Board. This suggests an important area to be examined in greater detail in future research.

For the purposes of this chapter, we will focus on apparent changes during the study period in certain patterns of PSRB decision making. We found little contribution to the increased hospital census observed during Time 3 from the two factors shown in Figure 5–4 (i.e., new admissions and revocations) that can cause an increase in hospitalization. When we looked at the decisions shown in Figure 5–5 that cause a decrease in hospital census (i.e., conditional releases and discharges), we found that both showed some relationship to the changes in the census, because both peaked in Time 2 and decreased in Time 3 and Time 4. However, only the rates of discretionary discharge significantly deviated from the expected rates. We believe that this phenomenon was thus the most significant single factor of the four factors that helps explain the observed changes in hospital census in Time 3.

At this point, we do not know what caused this change in the

PSRB's policy toward discretionary discharge. To date there are no studies of Board attitudes and decision making regarding discharge. We can thus only offer our speculation on what might have contributed to this change:

1. The PSRB, as one expects, experienced personnel changes during the 12-year study period. The Board has an executive director and five members appointed by the Governor for 4-year terms. During the 12-year study period, there were three executive directors and three to four different individuals in each of the five appointed Board positions. We do not know the extent to which these different persons, individually and as a group, had differing attitudes and developed different policies regarding discretionary discharges.

2. We do know that during Time 2, the Board discharged individuals who were thought to be inappropriate for PSRB jurisdiction. These individuals were primarily those diagnosed as having personality disorders (see Chapter 8). We know that certain hospital personnel believed that persons who primarily had personality disorders were inappropriate for the insanity defense and not treatable. These views resulted both in early discharge for some and in a 1983 revision of Oregon statutes to prohibit the use of the insanity defense by persons with illness "solely from a personality disorder" (8, 9). We recently evaluated the effectiveness of this statutory change (10) and found that individuals with personality disorder as their only diagnosis were apparently still being placed under Board jurisdiction by trial court judges. Individuals with personality disorders are thus still in the PSRB system and were being discharged in Time 3 as they were in Time 2.

3. Changes in Board actions may also reflect changes in societal attitudes concerning the insanity defense. After the 1982 insanity verdict in the case of John Hinckley, Jr., more attention was directed to the insanity defense, and there was increased pressure to restrict its use. Time 3 data might reflect a possible "Hinckley effect." The 1983 Oregon legislature was faced with several bills that attempted to severely restrict the insanity defense. These bills did not pass. However, it is possible that a message was given both to the hospital and to the PSRB re-

garding societal views about the insanity defense, insanity acquittees, and their release from the forensic inpatient setting.
4. Finally, judicial opinions may have resulted in a change in how the Board makes decisions. In 1985, the Oregon Court of Appeals reversed and remanded for trial a civil case against a community treatment agency involving a PSRB client who, while on conditional release, caused a fatal automobile accident (11) (see Chapter 4). The original trial court declared a summary judgment for the defendants, holding that they did not owe a duty to protect the driving public. The Court of Appeals reversed on the basis of the PSRB statutes, which hold societal protection as the primary concern of the Board. The Oregon Supreme Court affirmed the decision of the Court of Appeals. The case was eventually settled out of court. The influence of this case on the community mental health programs and on the decision making of the Board is not known. However, there were increased concerns in the community regarding potential liability for the actions of PSRB clients. Although this case was not heard in the Court of Appeals until 1985, it was in the trial courts before then, and its existence could have easily influenced the system even before a formal decision was made by the courts.

Thus, based on available data, we are unable to offer a precise explanation of the increase in hospital census in Time 3 and the subsequent stabilization in Time 4. There are a number of potential factors we cannot measure but that are likely to be related to the fluctuations in hospital census. For example, anecdotal information from the Board suggests that the number of discretionary discharges has increased recently and will continue to increase, because the Court of Appeals has issued a number of opinions in which it found that the Board lacked sufficient evidence to refuse a requested "discretionary discharge." These court opinions and the Board response to the opinions point to the fact that such discharges are not truly discretionary but, in fact, are mandated when an individual is found to be no longer mentally ill or no longer dangerous. In addition, the opinions and the increase in discretionary discharges demonstrate that the appellate courts continue to play an important role in defining the terms "no longer mentally ill" and "no longer dangerous" for the Board. However, the impact of these court opinions on Board actions is difficult to measure.

A careful examination of these suggested factors and other potential factors is needed to understand the increased hospital census observed in Time 3 and the subsequent plateau in Time 4. A steadily increasing hospital census is a threat to the entire innovative PSRB system. Increasing costs accompany an increased inpatient population, and costs for the hospital population are the most expensive in the system. Without a check on the inpatient population and the associated costs, we can expect greater demand for changes to reduce the numbers of persons admitted to the PSRB system. Over the years we have investigated a number of areas of the PSRB program. This is the first that reports a potentially serious system problem and threat to PSRB's overall stability. Given the changes between Time 3 and Time 4, the data in this chapter demonstrate the importance of continued monitoring of the PSRB system as it matures and responds to both internal and external influences.

REFERENCES

1. Steadman HJ, Monahan J, Hartstone E, et al: Mentally disordered offenders: a national survey of patients and facilities. Law and Human Behavior 6:31–38, 1982
2. Callahan LA, Steadman HJ, McGreevy MA, et al: The volume and characteristics of insanity defense pleas: an eight-state study. Bull Am Acad Psychiatry Law 19:331–338, 1991
3. Steadman HJ, Braff J: Defendants not guilty by reason of insanity, in Mentally Disordered Offenders: Perspectives From Law and Social Science. Edited by Monahan J, Steadman HJ. New York, Plenum, 1983, pp 109–129
4. Steadman HJ: Insanity defense research and treatment of insanity acquittees. Behavioral Sciences and the Law 3:37–48, 1985
5. Way BB, Dvoskin JA, Steadman HJ: Forensic psychiatric inpatients served in the United States: regional and system differences. Bull Am Acad Psychiatry Law 19:405–412, 1991

6. Rogers JL, Bloom JD, Manson SM: Oregon's new insanity defense system: a review of the first five years, 1978–1982. Bull Am Acad Psychiatry Law 12:383–402, 1984

7. Bigelow DA, Bloom JD, Williams MH: Costs of management and treatment of insanity acquittees under a Psychiatric Security Review Board system. Hosp Community Psychiatry 41:613–614, 1990

8. Oregon Revised Statutes, §161.295 (2)

9. Reynolds SE: Battle of the experts revisited: 1983 Oregon legislation on the insanity defense. Willamette Law Review 20:303–317, 1984

10. Reichlin SM, Bloom JD, Williams MH: Post-Hinckley insanity reform in Oregon. Bull Am Acad Psychiatry Law 18:405–413, 1990

11. Cain v Rijken, 74 Or. App. 76, 700 P.2d 1061 (1985); Cain v Rijken, 300 Or. 706, 717 P.2d 140 (1986)

Chapter 6

Community Treatment

I n this chapter, we focus on the community treatment of insanity acquittees. Chapter 4 described the hospitalization and conditional release of subjects while under Psychiatric Security Review Board (PSRB) jurisdiction. We found the system heavily weighted to inpatient care, with subjects spending 68% of their time under PSRB jurisdiction in the hospital. Individuals not conditionally released by the trial court judges had only a 40% chance of being conditionally released by the Board. However, even with this heavy reliance on inpatient care, 381 (50%) of the subjects experienced at least one conditional release.

We have identified the monitored community treatment of insanity acquittees as a particularly unique feature of the Oregon system, both in previous reports (1–3) and as a major theme of this book. As we emphasize in several chapters, the conditional release of insanity acquittees into monitored community programs is an area of growing national interest. In addition to describing the mechanisms that allow for the conditional release of insanity acquittees, the development of focused treatment programs for chronically mentally ill people contributes to effective community treatment programs for insanity acquittees (4). Oregon's insanity acquittees are predominantly chronically mentally ill individuals, who most frequently have schizophrenia, and who have substantial past experience in both the mental health and criminal justice systems. Other jurisdictions have reported similar characteristics for insanity acquittees (5, 6). Given these characteristics, treatment programs similar to those developed for chronically mentally ill people that emphasize community support, case management, and medication management (7,

The authors wish to thank Jo Mahler, M.S., for her extensive contribution to this chapter.

8) provide appropriate models for the monitored community treatment programs for insanity acquittees.

As we discussed in Chapter 1, the history of community mental health services for chronically mentally ill citizens in Oregon paralleled developments on the federal level (9, 10). In 1981, the legislature reorganized Oregon's community mental health program and made treatment of chronically mentally ill citizens the highest priority of the community mental health system. These revisions organized community mental health services into service elements and made the community treatment of insanity acquittees a separate service element.

In this chapter, we describe services provided to insanity acquittees in monitored community treatment programs, report on acquittee satisfaction with these community services, and describe problems that acquittees experienced while they were in the community.

Data for this chapter come primarily from two of the data bases described in Chapter 3: the Community Program Record and the Community Interview. These data bases contain information on male subjects who had a working diagnosis of psychosis and whom Oregon judges placed under PSRB jurisdiction following felony range crimes. The Community Program Record Data Base contains information derived from record reviews of community mental health files on 93 male subjects on conditional release to one of Oregon's three largest community treatment programs for PSRB clients. The Community Interview Data Base contains information derived from serial interviews of 54 males whom we interviewed every 3 months for up to 2 years. We completed a total of 248 interviews on these 54 subjects, as well as 246 interviews with their case managers. It should be noted that some of the subjects included in this data base were assigned to the Board's jurisdiction after 1986 and thus should be considered additions to the 758 subjects who form the core sample for this book.

Some additional data came from the PSRB Record Data Base, which contains information from the monthly reports that community case managers submitted to the PSRB. This data base contains information on the 381 individuals conditionally released during the study period.

THE CONDITIONAL RELEASE PLAN

As described in detail in Chapter 1, conditional release is controlled by a plan agreed to by the Board, the community treatment program, and the individual insanity acquittee. Table 6–1 provides a summary of the various conditions that appeared in a review of the conditional release plans for the 381 subjects conditionally released during the study period. The most frequently occurring conditions specified the mental health treatment program responsible for monitoring the conditionally released subject and addressed the question of housing. These were followed by additional requirements stipulating the continuation of psychotropic medication and prohibiting the use of alcohol and drugs. The large "other" category contained special conditions, such as a prohibition on family visits without prior approval of the case manager.

COMMUNITY SERVICES

The Community Program Record Data Base contains data on 93 subjects who experienced 159 separate conditional release epi-

Table 6–1.   Legal conditions for conditional release plan (from the PSRB Record Data Base; $N = 381$)

Condition	n	%
Mental health treatment	338	89
Housing	305	80
Medication	171	45
Alcohol/drugs restricted	126	33
Driving restricted	54	14
Drug screens	46	12
Employment	44	12
Antabuse	31	8
Alcohol/drug treatment	22	6
Day program	7	2
Travel restricted	5	1
Other	75	20

sodes. Service data are presented for these 93 subjects by combining the services they received across these 159 conditional release episodes. Ninety-eight percent of the subjects received mental health evaluation and treatment services. In addition to these basic mental health services, 87% of subjects received some form of income support, 70% received services from a day treatment program, and 68% lived in one or more structured residences at some point during their conditional release episodes. Fifty-eight percent of the sample received medical and/or dental health services, and 47% received vocational or educational services. Legal issues continued to be important in the lives of these individuals, with 61% receiving these services during their conditional release. Legal services provided to these subjects were predominantly for representation at Board hearings and/or appeals of Board orders.

Table 6–2 presents data from both the Community Program Record and the Community Interview data bases that provide greater detail about the types of mental health treatment provided to subjects. The first section of the table lists services provided to the 93 conditionally released subjects and depicts the average number of times per month that each subject received these services. The second section specifies services rendered to the 54 subjects in the interview sample. Data from case manager interviews are also included in this second section. To simplify the table, the second section contains only summary information.

Ninety-seven percent of the 93 subjects described in the first section had individual sessions with mental health professionals (usually their case manager) an average of three times per month. Ninety-five percent had medication evaluation and prescriptions once a month; 75% of subjects were visited in their residences or had some other form of outreach service on a once-monthly basis. The 59% of the subjects who received group sessions participated in groups slightly more frequently than on a weekly basis. Other services such as family counseling and substance abuse treatment were received on a far less frequent basis by far fewer subjects.

Referring to the second section, the 54 subjects in the interview sample received similar services. For this data base, we coded individual sessions as case management services, and 96% of the sample received such services. A large number of subjects (94%) also received medication services. Group counseling was reported with similar frequency in the two data bases, whereas family counseling was reported at 24% in one sample and 9% in the other.

Table 6–2. Mental health treatment provided to conditionally released subjects ($N = 93$)

Treatment services	n	%	n per month
Community Record Review Data Base ($N = 93$)			
Individual sessions	90	97	2.86
Medication evaluation/prescription	88	95	0.97
Home visit/outreach	70	75	1.04
Administration/monitoring medication	58	62	0.61
Group sessions	55	59	4.20
Urinalysis	39	42	0.68
Medication laboratory tests	30	32	0.44
Family sessions	22	24	0.20
Alcohol/drug treatment	11	12	0.49
Crisis intervention	6	6	0.04
Community Interview Data Base ($N = 54$)			
Case management (office)		96	
Case management (outreach)		52	
Medications		94	
Psychiatric evaluation		91	
Individual counseling		57	
Group counseling		56	
Family counseling		9	
Activity programs (day treatment)		76	
Activities of daily living training		48	
Social skills training		43	
Vocational training		44	
Crisis intervention		15	
Substance Abuse Services			
Urine monitoring		59	
Drug/alcohol counseling		35	
Antabuse		13	

In the interview sample, we have a better assessment of the types of services most often associated with community support services. Seventy-six percent of subjects experienced placement in day treatment programs, whereas fewer than 50% of the subjects in the sample received special training in activities of daily living, social skills, or vocational training. Emphasis on the detection of substance abuse through urine monitoring occurred much more frequently than specific substance abuse counseling.

Table 6–3, derived from the Community Program Record Data Base, lists the mental health professionals who provided the services to these 93 subjects. Psychiatrists, case managers, workers concerned with income support, other mental health workers, and residential staff provided most of the services. Legal workers, physical health providers, and vocational counselors had less involvement with subjects.

As noted from Table 6–1, housing is an important component of the conditional release plan, because 80% of conditional release plans contained a provision relating to housing. Table 6–4 categorizes the various residential settings for the 93 subjects during their conditional release. It was not uncommon for subjects to change their residential placement during a single conditional release episode. Thus, the number of placements in this table is larger than the total number of subjects. Table 6–4

Table 6–3.   Providers of services (from the Community Record Data Base; $N = 93$)

Provider	n	%
Psychiatrist	87	94
Case manager	84	90
Income support agency staff	76	82
Other mental health worker	68	73
Residential staff	67	72
Legal workers	50	54
Physical health provider	49	53
Vocational/occupation program staff	48	52
Nurse	29	31
Corrections supervisors	9	10

illustrates the importance of structured residential placements for this population. Sixty-eight percent of the 93 subjects spent some time in structured residential settings, the most common of which were group homes. Structured housing represents 48% of the total placements for the sample. Fifty-six percent of the subjects spent some time in various types of independent living situations, whereas 18% spent time in family settings.

CLIENT SATISFACTION

We derived information on subject satisfaction with various aspects of their conditional release program from the Community Interview Data Base. Thirty-six percent of the subjects in this sample thought that the quality of the services offered was excellent, and 50% thought that it was good. Forty-three percent thought that the services helped them a great deal, while another 43% thought that they were helped somewhat in dealing with their problems. Even with these generally positive feelings, 43% of those interviewed said that they would not voluntarily partic-

Table 6–4. Residential placements treatment sample ($N = 93$)

Residential placement	n	% of N Subjects	% of Total placements
Structured settings	63	68	48
Group home	55	59	32
Other structured setting	14	15	8
Satellite apartment	13	14	7
Semi-independent living	8	9	5
Adult foster care	5	5	3
Nursing home	1	1	1
Unsupported residential	52	56	39
Independent living	47	51	27
Room and board	11	12	6
Other unsupported	2	2	1
Family settings	17	18	13
Parents	8	9	5
Spouse and/or children	6	6	3
Other family	4	4	2

ipate in the program if it were not required, whereas 57% said that they would participate voluntarily in a program similar to their current program.

Case managers viewed the effects of their services on clients in a positive light. They thought that their services were very helpful for 67% of the subjects and of some help for 25%, and not helpful in only 8% of the cases.

Case manager and subject perceptions were much more divergent regarding psychiatric medications. Fifty-two percent of the subjects found medications were very helpful, 19% found them to be of some help, and 29% thought that they were of no help. This is in marked contrast to the case managers, who thought that medications were very helpful in 92% of cases and of no help to only one person.

Seventy-four percent of subjects were satisfied with the physical conditions of their living situation, 17% were neutral, and 9% expressed dissatisfaction. Eighty-nine percent were satisfied with the amount of privacy that was available to them, and 87% were satisfied with the amount of physical space available to them in their housing situations.

PROBLEMS EXPERIENCED BY CLIENTS ON CONDITIONAL RELEASE

We have examined problems experienced by subjects while on conditional release by reviewing monthly case manager reports to the PSRB about subjects' adjustment to conditional release and by interviewing case managers and subjects regarding problems experienced during conditional release.

The PSRB Record Data Base summarized the periodic reports made to the PSRB by community case managers on the 381 conditionally released subjects who experienced a total of 561 conditional release episodes. Of these 381 subjects, 346 subjects had monthly reports available in the PSRB files. Table 6–5 lists the problems that case managers reported to the PSRB for these 346 subjects and the percentage of the reports in which these problems were listed. The most frequently reported problems were concerns about the subject's mental condition, appearing in 43%

of the reports. This was followed by problems related to the mental health treatment situation, difficulties in the subject's interpersonal relationships, work-related problems, housing, and physical health concerns. Reports seldom mentioned problems regarding substance abuse and legal problems. It is also of interest, given the reported divergence of perception about the helpfulness of psychotropic medications mentioned previously, that problems with medications appeared in only 4% of the reports.

We also derived data on problems experienced by subjects in the community from the Community Interview Data Base. We asked the case managers of the 54 subjects to report on the severity of problems that each of the subjects experienced in the 3-month interval between interviews. Problems were rated as "none or only minor," "significant," or "extreme." Significant and extreme problems were reported on a relatively infrequent basis. Case managers reported significant problems in the area of compliance with the treatment plan in only 5% of reports. These included problems with keeping appointments and taking medications. Although case managers did not frequently report lack of compliance as a significant problem, they did report concerns

Table 6–5. Problems reported for conditionally released subjects (from the PSRB Record Data Base; N = 346)

Problem	n	% of N	% of Reports
Mental health condition	281	80	43
Mental health treatment	238	68	26
Interpersonal	173	50	15
Housing	173	50	14
Working	150	43	15
Health	138	40	10
Alcohol/drugs	108	31	6
Finances	104	30	6
Medications	92	26	4
Legal	30	9	1
Meaningful use of time	30	9	1
Driving	18	5	1
Training	12	3	< 1

with the various subjects' mental condition. In 17% of the interviews, case managers reported significant problems in the client's mental condition during the preceding 3 months. In 1% of the interviews, case managers rated these problems as extreme. The highest response rating ever reported for problems with substance abuse was "significant" in 8% of interviews. Extreme problems with substance abuse were never reported by case managers. There was also a relative paucity of dangerous behavior reported from the interviews. Case managers and subjects reported threatening behaviors or displays and dangerous family conflicts in 10% and 6%, respectively, of the interviews, whereas they reported property damage in 2% of the interviews. They reported other dangerous behaviors including assaultive behavior in 4% of the interviews and suicidal risk in 4% of the interviews. Case managers reported legal contacts and/or criminal charges for four subjects.

An area of significant interest was subjects' use of time, including current employment or student status, future plans for work and/or school, and the appraisal by subjects and case managers of time spent on conditional release. Thirty percent of subjects were employed in either full-time or part-time jobs or were placed in a sheltered workplace setting, while 57% were unemployed. Six percent were in school. Forty-one percent of subjects had no concrete plans for the future.

Subjects' use of time, as viewed by both the subjects themselves and by case managers, was problematic. Seventeen percent of subjects reported poor use of their time on conditional release, while another 20% reported only adequate use of time. Case managers reported significant problems with use of time for 27% of the cases and extreme problems for 2% of the cases at least once during the study period.

Sixteen (30%) of the 54 subjects in the community interview sample were rehospitalized during the study period. The PSRB formally revoked 12 (22%) of the rehospitalized subjects. The most frequent reason(s) given by case managers for these revocations included refusal to follow the treatment plan, substance use, and mental decompensation. Case managers reported dangerousness as a primary reason for revocation in three cases.

DISCUSSION

Data presented in this chapter focused on several key areas in the community treatment of conditionally released insanity acquittees, including the conditional release plan, the services provided in the community, subject satisfaction with community placement, and the problems subjects experienced during conditional release.

We described statutory ground rules for conditional release in Chapter 1 and presented a typical conditional release plan developed by the Board. From the data presented in this chapter, the PSRB most frequently designated the mental health program that would administer the conditional release, named the case manager who would report on a monthly basis, and specified the initial housing placement for the conditionally released person. About one-half of the subjects' plans had conditions related to psychotropic medications. Concerns about substance abuse were evident in the plans we reviewed. About one-third of the plans restricted the use of alcohol and/or drugs. Other concerns about substance abuse were reflected in the conditions that ordered drug screens, Antabuse treatment, and/or specific alcohol and drug abuse treatment.

Fourteen percent of the plans contained driving restrictions. This was less than anticipated, given the high visibility of *Cain v. Rijken* (11). As described in Chapter 4, this case involved a conditionally released individual whose reckless driving caused the death of two other drivers. This case generated a great deal of concern about the driving of mentally ill individuals (12). However, this case was not reported until 1986, the year that our study period ended. It is likely that a more recent sampling of conditional release plans would include a greater frequency of driving restrictions.

Once in the community, subjects received an array of services consistent with a community support model for chronically mentally ill people. By combining the data from our review of community records with data generated from interviews of subjects, we get a picture of the types of services provided. It should be remembered that we sampled males, diagnosed as having some form of psychosis, who were committed to the jurisdiction of the

PSRB following felony crimes. We elected to focus on these subjects, because they are representative of the bulk of Oregon's insanity acquittees. As we demonstrate in other chapters in this book, women and misdemeanants have unique careers under the PSRB. The same can be said of subjects who are diagnosed primarily with character disorders or mental retardation and who are described in Chapter 8.

As expected, almost all of these psychotic male subjects received mental health treatment mediated by case managers. Case managers also provided outreach services for 75% of the record review sample and 52% of the interview sample. Psychiatrists were also involved with most subjects, and medications were used in 94% of cases. In addition, subjects frequently received both residential and day treatment services.

Aside from the counseling associated with case management, more formal individual, group, and family therapy were used less frequently. In addition, the specific focus on skills building—including training in activities of daily living, social skills development, and vocational training—were applied to fewer than half of the subjects. Substance abuse services appeared to consist more of monitoring than of counseling subjects.

Other services were important to this group of subjects. A large majority received some type of income support, and 61% received legal supportive services. Particularly noteworthy was that more than 50% were treated for physical and/or dental problems. Physical health care appeared to be oriented toward acute problems rather to longitudinal and/or preventive care. These data suggest the need for further work in this area, given the developing literature on the medical needs of chronically mentally ill people (13, 14). The data suggest undertreatment of the medical and dental needs of this chronically ill population. Community mental health programs in Oregon have reported difficulties in arranging for the medical care of their clients (15). We assume that these problems also exist in other jurisdictions.

In addition to the types of services received by subjects on conditional release, we have data on the frequency that subjects received these services. Subjects who received individual sessions averaged about three sessions per month. In addition, they had a home visit or some type of outreach service once a month and also received medication services once a month. Those subjects who received group therapy attended slightly more than four groups per month. Although 42% received some type of urine monitoring for substance abuse, this was done less frequently than once a month. Crisis intervention occurred infrequently. It is possible that case managers resolved crises more often by revocation than by attempts at crisis resolution in the community. This hypothesis needs further exploration.

Housing is a critical component of any program dealing with chronically mentally ill people (16, 17). It is even more of an issue in relation to the community placement of chronically ill insanity acquittees (18). Having structured residential placements available is, in fact, a rate-limiting factor in the conditional release of insanity acquittees. Overcoming barriers to the community housing of insanity acquittees is even more of a challenge than it is in planning appropriate housing for the chronically mentally ill population in general (19).

Our data highlight the significance of housing to the process of conditional release in Oregon. Eighty percent of conditional release plans contained a provision related to housing. Furthermore, close to 70% of the subjects in our sample lived in some form of structured housing at some point during their conditional release. Case managers frequently mentioned housing as a concern in the monthly reports to the PSRB; they listed housing specifically in 14% of their reports. It is also important to note the level of continuing contact with the families of insanity acquittees. As we reported in Chapter 3, the population of Oregon's insanity acquittees is generally older and unmarried; yet families provided housing for about 20% of insanity acquittees at some point during their conditional release. Our work suggest the need for more studies of the family relationships of these seriously ill insanity acquittees (20).

We considered subjects' satisfaction with their conditional release programs as related to the important question of quality of life for these conditionally released individuals (21). Areas of concern in relation to quality of life included meaningful use of time, current employment or schooling, and plans for the future. In these areas, subjects' use of time for productive activities was problematic.

Subjects viewed the overall treatment offered to them in a very positive light, but slightly fewer than half stated they would not participate in a similar treatment program on a strictly voluntary basis. Case managers also felt that the services offered were very positive for the subjects. Subjects were generally quite satisfied with their living situation, their private space, and the respect of their privacy. The largest divergence of views between subjects and case managers came in relation to medications. Case managers thought that medications were much more helpful than did the subjects.

Subject reports about whether they would continue to participate in a voluntary treatment program similar to what was provided under the auspices of the Board, and their views of the necessity of psychotropic medication, may offer some clues about how these subjects view their illnesses. In other sections of this book, we discussed the fact that subjects had frequent involuntary psychiatric hospitalizations both prior to and following PSRB jurisdiction. One might postulate that insanity acquittees represent a subgroup of the chronically mentally ill population with particularly limited insight into the nature of their illnesses. As a result, they find themselves involved more frequently in an involuntary relationship with the civil commitment or criminal justice systems. This may be in marked contrast to chronically mentally ill people who may understand their illnesses better and seek and accept treatment when symptoms reoccur. Insight into mental illness has been shown to be a critical factor in treatment refusal (22). We have postulated similar factors in relation to the treatment refusal of insanity acquittees (23), and we are currently investigating this area further.

Finally, as we discussed in Chapter 4, we were very interested in obtaining some assessment of whether revocation may have taken place too quickly before community programs were able to make sufficient attempts to resolve crises in the community. The small number of revocations in the community interview sample did not allow us to conclusively examine this question. Only 12 of the 54 subjects had a formal revocation during the 2-year period. The primary reasons for these revocations included failure to follow the treatment plan, the use of alcohol or drugs, and/or the exacerbation of mental symptoms. Actual dangerous behavior was a primary reason for revocation for only 3 subjects. These data support the impression that the case managers followed statutory guidelines that allow revocation of conditional release for violations of the conditional release plan and/or deterioration in the subject's mental condition. As conditional release becomes more popular and more jurisdictions adopt such programs, we expect that there will be an opportunity to examine the revocation process further.

In conclusion, although we examined the conditional release program only for male psychotic felons, these subjects received treatment in community programs using a community support model similar to what has been developed for nonforensic chronically mentally ill populations. The data presented in this chapter demonstrate that these programs can be adapted for a forensic population and that both clients and treatment providers are generally satisfied with the results.

REFERENCES

1. Rogers JL, Bloom JD, Manson SM: Oregon's Psychiatric Security Review Board: a comprehensive system for managing insanity acquittees, in Mental Health and Law: Research and Policy. Annals of the American Academy of Political and Social Sciences 484:86–99, 1986
2. Bloom JD, Bradford J, Kofoed L: An overview of the psychiatric treatment of certain offender groups. Hosp Community Psychiatry 39:151–159, 1988
3. Bloom JD, Williams MH, Rogers JL, et al: Evaluation and treatment of insanity acquittees in the community. Bull Am Acad Psychiatry Law 14:231–244, 1986
4. Bloom JD, Williams MH, Bigelow DA: Monitored conditional release of persons found not guilty by reason of insanity. Am J Psychiatry 148:444–448, 1991
5. Petrilla J: The insanity defense and other mental health dispositions in Missouri. Int J Law Psychiatry 5:81–101, 1982
6. McGreevy MA, Steadman HJ, Callahan LA: The negligible effects of California's 1982 reform of the insanity defense test. Am J Psychiatry 148:744–750, 1991

7. Lamb HR, Treating the Long-Term Mentally Ill: Beyond Deinstitutionalization. San Francisco, CA, Jossey-Bass, 1983

8. Talbott JA: The Chronic Mental Patient—Five Years Later. New York, Grune & Stratton, 1984

9. Bloom JD, Cutler DL, Faulkner LR, et al: The evolution of Oregon's public psychiatry training program. New Dir Ment Health Serv 44:113–121, 1989

10. Foley HA, Sharfstein SS: Madness and Government: Who Cares for the Mentally Ill? Washington, DC, American Psychiatric Press, 1983

11. Cain v Rijken, 717 P.2d 140, 300 Ore 706, 1986

12. Godard SL, Bloom JD: Driving, mental illness, and the duty to protect, in Confidentiality Versus the Duty to Protect. Edited by Beck JC. Washington, DC, American Psychiatric Press, 1990, pp 191–204

13. Maricle RA, Hoffman WF, Faulkner LR, et al: The coexistence of physical and mental illness among two samples of Oregon's chronically mentally ill. New Dir Ment Health Serv 44:97–110, 1989

14. Farmer S: Medical problems of chronic patients in a community support program. Hosp Community Psychiatry 38:745–749, 1987

15. Faulkner LR, Bloom JD, Maricle BM: Medical services in Oregon's Community Mental Health Programs. Hosp Community Psychiatry 37:1045–1047, 1986

16. Cutler DL: Community residential options for the chronically mentally ill. Community Ment Health J 22:61–73, 1986

17. Baker F, Douglas C: Housing environments and community adjustment of severely mentally ill persons. Community Ment Health J 26:497–505, 1990

18. Goldmeier J, Sauer RH, White EV: A half-way house for mentally ill offenders. Am J Psychiatry 34:45–49, 1977

19. Wenocur S, Belcher JR: Strategies for overcoming barriers to community-based housing for the chronically mentally ill. Community Ment Health J 26:319–333

20. McFarland BH, Faulkner LR, Bloom JD, et al: Chronic mental illness and the criminal justice system. Hosp Community Psychiatry 40:718–724, 1989

21. Bigelow DA, McFarland BH, Olson MM: Quality of life of community mental health program clients: validating a measure. Community Ment Health J 27:43–55, 1991

22. Schwartz HI, Vingiano W, Perez CB: Autonomy and the right to refuse treatment: patient's attitudes after involuntary medication. Hosp Community Psychiatry 39:1049–1054, 1988

23. Williams MH, Bloom JD, Faulkner LR, et al: Treatment refusal and length of hospitalization of insanity acquittees. Bull Am Acad Psychiatry Law 16:279–285, 1988

Chapter 7

Insanity Acquittees
After Psychiatric
Security Review
Board Jurisdiction

There is very little systematic follow-up information on what happens to insanity acquittees after their release from the jurisdiction of courts or supervisory bodies such as the Psychiatric Security Review Board (PSRB). There are some former insanity acquittees who come to the attention of the general public through the commission of new crimes. These events often become highly sensationalized when it is learned that the individual had previously "gotten off" with an insanity verdict (1, 2).

Much of the research that has been done in this area has focused on the rehospitalization and the rearrest of released acquittees. Earlier review articles by Pasewark in 1981 (3), and Steadman and Braff in 1983 (4), provided some initial information on the these two outcome measures. Rehospitalization rates in two studies were reported at 22% and 37% and rearrests in three studies with small numbers of insanity acquittees ranged from 15% to 65%.

Three studies from Maryland have added to the information provided by these earlier reviews. The first (5) examined the arrest rates of 86 insanity acquittees for up to 15 years following their discharge from the psychiatric hospitalization resulting from a successful insanity verdict. Fifty-six percent were arrested during this extended follow-up period. In a subsequent study (6), the authors examined the hospitalization and arrests of insanity acquittees both before and after discharge from the index hospitalization and compared these insanity acquittees with offenders released from prison. Forty-six percent of the insanity acquittees were rehospitalized and 66% were rearrested during an extensive follow-up period that averaged 10 years. Rearrests grew from 23% at the end of 1 year to 66% at the end of 10 years. After 10 years, the rates plateaued. The authors demonstrated the importance of the length of the follow-up period in determining the arrest rates of former insanity acquittees. The third study (7) compared insanity acquittees discharged from the state forensic hospital with those discharged from regional psychiatric facilities and followed these individuals for 5 years after hospital discharge. Sixty-four percent of those discharged from the forensic hospital and 79% of those discharged from the regional hospital were rehospitalized in the follow-up period, whereas 47% of the forensic hospital group and 63% of the regionalized patients were rearrested among the outcome measures.

A recent study from California (8) compared hospitalization and arrests for those who were conditionally released and those who were discharged from a forensic hospital with no conditional release. Both groups consisted primarily of insanity acquittees. The finding in relation to the conditional release group was described in Chapter 4. Of those discharged with no conditional release, 27% were arrested and 9% hospitalized during the 2-year follow-up period.

We reported (9) on the rearrest of 41% of 123 insanity acquittees released from PSRB jurisdiction in the first 3 years of PSRB operation (1978–1980). Because the Board released subjects from their jurisdiction at different times during 1978–1980, follow-up time in this study varied from 2 to 5 years. Subjects had a mean of 1.2 arrests per person and 77% of first arrests took place within the first year after discharge. This chapter expands on the information available in this earlier article by examining mental health and criminal justice system contacts of insanity acquittees after PSRB discharge.

This chapter describes the arrests and hospitalization of discharged insanity acquittees. In addition, we explore two other areas. The first relates to the question of prediction of dangerousness as we compare mandatory and discretionary discharges. The second focuses on the critical question of the adjustment of discharged insanity acquittees.

METHODOLOGY

As discussed in Chapter 1, the Board discharges an insanity acquittee from its jurisdiction either at the completion of the insanity sentence imposed by the trial court judge or, prior to the end of the insanity sentence, when the Board concludes that an individual is no longer mentally ill and/or no longer dangerous. We have called these two types of discharges mandatory and discretionary discharge. After discharge, unless the state institutes civil commitment proceedings, individuals are free of all restraints that characterized their time under the Board's jurisdiction.

Of the 758 subjects in the study, the Board discharged 422 (56%) during the study period. This chapter begins with a description of these 422 discharged subjects and their mental health and criminal justice system involvement after their discharge from PSRB jurisdiction. We then examine the question of the prediction of dangerousness and the adjustment of discharged insanity acquittees.

STUDY 1:
SUBJECTS DISCHARGED
FROM PSRB JURISDICTION

As stated, during the study period 1978–1986, the Board discharged 422 individuals or 56% of the 758 subjects in our research sample. Of these 422 individuals, the Board discharged 222 subjects (53%) because the Board found them to be no longer mentally ill and/or no longer dangerous, and discharged 170 (40%) because the maximum length of PSRB jurisdiction elapsed. An additional 21 subjects died while under the Board's jurisdiction, 8 from natural causes and 13 from suicide. The Oregon Court of Appeals ordered 2% of the subjects discharged for various reasons including reversal of their convictions or the Board's failure to hold mandatory hearings.

The discharged sample included 182 misdemeanants, representing 43% of the discharge sample. This is much larger than the 27% of misdemeanants who composed the admission sample of

758 subjects. An additional 144 subjects or 34% of those discharged, had been assigned by trial court judges for 5-year insanity sentences. These were expected findings since the jurisdictional time of misdemeanants is limited to 1 year and those whom the courts assigned to PSRB jurisdiction for 5 years between 1978–1981 would have had mandatory discharges during the study period.

During the study period the Board discharged 24% of the sample who had longer PSRB jurisdictional terms: 8% (n = 32) with 10-year terms; 14% (n = 60) with 20-year terms, and 2% (n = 10) with 40 or more years for their insanity sentence. Because the length of the study period was 9 years, all of these subjects had discretionary discharges, unless, as mentioned, discharge occurred on order of the Court of Appeals, or as a result of a subject's death.

Sixty-five percent of subjects were discharged from the hospital and 35% were discharged from conditional release. Of the subjects with discretionary discharges, 75% were discharged from the hospital and 25% were discharged from community placements. This is significantly different from percentages for subjects who had mandatory discharges in which 55% were discharged from the hospital and 45% were discharged from the community (χ^2 = 18.859, df = 1, P = .0000).

Although we have pointed to a sex difference in several chapters in this book, the overall discharge cohort contains the same proportions of men (87%) and women (13%) as the entry cohort.

Table 7–1 presents the year of PSRB discharge for the 422 discharged subjects. In its first 2 years, the Board discharged relatively few subjects (i.e., 9% of the discharge sample). During the next 3 years, 1980–1982, the Board discharged 48% of the sample, whereas in the last 4 years of the study period, 1983–1986, the Board discharged 44% of the sample. We examined the differences in the various types of discharges across a 12-year time period in Chapter 5.

Table 7–1 also indirectly demonstrates that the length of follow-up time depends on the date of discharge. The average follow-up time was 53 months. Only 11% of the sample had fewer than 18 months of follow-up during the study period.

Involvement of Discharged Insanity Acquittees in the Mental Health and Criminal Justice Systems

To create a more meaningful sample to examine the involvement of discharged subjects in the mental health and criminal justice systems, we subtracted the 21 subjects who died while under PSRB jurisdiction and also subtracted those subjects whom the Board released in the last 6 months of 1986. This produced a sample of 381 and allowed for a minimum follow-up period of at least 6 months. To place our findings in context, we compared them with subjects' prior behavior. Data is thus presented for subjects' involvement in the mental health and criminal justice systems both before and after PSRB jurisdiction.

Following discharge, 65% of the 381 subjects were hospitalized at least once, 50% had at least one criminal justice contact and 40% had involvement with both systems. Twenty-five percent of the sample had no involvement with either system after discharge from PSRB jurisdiction. These findings are significantly influenced by the length of follow-up time. Those with contacts, with either the mental health or criminal justice systems, had a mean of 4.8 years of follow-up time compared to 3.2 years for those subjects with no contacts ($t = 7.128$, $df = 374$, $P = .0000$). Fifty-two percent of first arrests took place in the first year after the Board discharged the subject, while 70% took place in the first 18 months.

Table 7-1. Year of discharge from the PSRB ($N = 422$)

Year	Number discharged	%
1978	5	1
1979	32	8
1980	63	15
1981	62	15
1982	74	18
1983	55	13
1984	37	9
1985	46	11
1986	48	11

The 65% of those subjects hospitalized after discharge compares to 74% of the sample who were hospitalized at some point prior to PSRB jurisdiction. Subjects had a mean of 2.85 hospitalizations before PSRB jurisdiction compared to 2.13 hospitalizations after discharge from PSRB jurisdiction.

Table 7–2 provides a comparison of the relationship of psychiatric hospitalization and criminal justice involvement before and after PSRB jurisdiction. There were significant differences in each area. The largest percentage of subjects demonstrate contacts in both time periods. Fifty-two percent of the sample had involvement with the mental health system and 43% with the criminal justice system both before and after assignment to PSRB jurisdiction. When we combined mental health and criminal justice system involvement, 28% of the sample had involvement in both systems before and after PSRB, while only 4% had no involvement in either system before and after PSRB. Again, as indicated in Table 7–2, those subjects with contacts in either the mental health or the criminal justice system had a significantly longer time in follow-up.

Table 7–2. Mental health and criminal justice comparison before and after PSRB ($N = 381$)

	Involvement post-PSRB	
	No	Yes
Mental health system involvement[a]		
Involvement pre-PSRB		
No	47 (12%)	51 (13%)
Yes	85 (22%)	198 (52%)
Follow-up in years[b]	3.58	4.84
Criminal justice system involvement[c]		
Involvement pre-PSRB		
No	49 (13%)	25 (7%)
Yes	142 (37%)	165 (43%)
Follow-up in years[d]	3.81	5.04

[a] $\chi^2 = 10.33$, df = 1, $P = .0013$.
[b] $t = 6.00$, df = 379, $P = .0000$.
[c] $\chi = 9.504$, df = 1, $P = .0020$.
[d] $t = 6.20$, df = 374, $P = .0000$.

Table 7–3 depicts criminal justice contacts before and after PSRB jurisdiction. The average number of these contacts decreased significantly from 4.2 per subject to 1.4 per subject ($t = 18.1$, df $= 380$, $P = .0000$) We also found a significant decrease in numbers of criminal contacts when we corrected these rates of contacts for length of follow-up time. The average criminal contact decreased from 0.5 per year to 0.3 per year ($t = 5.2$, df $= 377$, $P = .0000$). In addition, there was a significant shift in the follow-

Table 7–3.   Criminal justice contacts before and after PSRB

Crime category	Before PSRB		After PSRB	
	Frequency	**%**	**Frequency**	**%**
Felony crimes	616	48	215	40
Burglary	118	9	47	9
Assault	105	8	28	5
Drug offenses	90	7	8	1
Theft	76	6	21	4
Escape/failure to appear	42	3	21	4
Unauthorized use of auto	39	3	21	4
Criminal mischief	36	3	24	4
Robbery	36	3	11	2
Arson	16	1	5	1
Sexual assault	14	1	12	2
Driving offenses	7	1	5	1
Homicide	6	< 1	—	—
Kidnapping	3	< 1	2	< 1
Weapons offenses	2	< 1	—	—
Other felony	26	2	10	2
Misdemeanor crimes	669	52	319	60
Theft	207	16	98	18
Driving offenses	98	8	36	7
Trespass	93	7	54	10
Resisting arrest	76	6	16	3
Menacing/harassment	73	6	66	12
Criminal mischief	30	2	9	2
Sexual offenses	33	3	17	3
Weapons offenses	19	1	8	1
Escape/failure to appear	16	1	12	2
Arson	6	< 1	1	< 1
Other misdemeanor	18	2	2	< 1

up period to less serious crimes as illustrated in the significant increase in the proportions of misdemeanors to felonies (χ^2 = 8.957, df = 1, P = .0028) and in the difference in the mean seriousness score of these crimes from 463 in the pre-PSRB time period to 494 in the follow-up period (t = 3.5, df = 377, P = .0005).

In addition to these changes in the number and seriousness of crimes in the follow-up period, we also found a significant relationship between those who had arrests in the pre- and post-PSRB time periods. This relationship is illustrated in the correlation between the number of criminal contacts in the time periods prior to and following discharge from PSRB (χ^2 = 0.31, df = 379, P = .0000) and in the data presented in Table 7–2.

STUDY 2: COMPARISON OF SUBJECTS WITH MANDATORY AND DISCRETIONARY DISCHARGES

This study examines the question of the relationship between the type of discharge and the involvement of discharged subjects in the mental health and criminal justice systems. As described in Chapter 3, the Mental Health Data Base contains information on psychiatric hospitalization in state facilities dating back to the 1950s, with considerably increased reliability from the 1970s forward. We were able to obtain reliable data on community psychiatric contacts dating from 1980. Because of the differences in the reliability of hospital and community data and in order to include community data in our analyses, we chose to examine a group of 252 subjects discharged between 1981 and 1985. The use of this sample allowed us to look at a group of subjects during a period of time when we had reliable community data, and for whom we had at least 1 year of follow-up data after discharge from PSRB jurisdiction.

The sample for this study consisted of 104 (41%) subjects whom the Board discharged when their maximum period of jurisdiction ran out, 114 (45%) subjects discharged as no longer dangerous, and 34 (14%) subjects discharged as no longer mentally ill. There were no differences between the groups in relation to demographic variables. Table 7–4 shows the relative proportions of mandatory and discretionary discharges that make up this discharge sample across discharge years. As can be seen from the table, there was a dramatic shift in the makeup of these yearly discharge cohorts in 1983 with a shift from predominantly discretionary to predominantly mandatory discharges (see Chapter 5). As illustrated in Table 7–5, we found differences among the three groups in relation to the length of assignment to PSRB jurisdiction. As expected, all subjects who were discharged because their PSRB jurisdiction elapsed had been assigned to the PSRB by the courts for 5 years or less. There were very different patterns in the relationship between length of assignment and the two types of discretionary discharges. Most of the discretionary

Table 7–4.   Discharge year and type of discharge ($N = 252$)

Discharge year	Jurisdiction elapsed ($N =104$)		No longer ill ($N = 34$)		No longer dangerous ($N = 114$)	
	n	%	n	%	n	%
1981	18	30	7	21	35	70
1982	15	21	15	44	40	79
1983	29	60	5	15	14	40
1984	22	63	4	12	9	37
1985	20	51	3	9	16	49

Note. $\chi^2 = 32.833$, df = 8, $P = .0001$.

Table 7–5.   Length of assignment to PSRB jurisdiction ($N = 252$)

Length of assignment (years)	Jurisdiction elapsed ($N = 104$)		No longer ill ($N = 34$)		No longer dangerous ($N = 114$)	
	n	%	n	%	n	%
1	68	65	3	9	26	23
5	36	35	8	24	51	45
10	—		6	18	12	10
20	—		12	35	22	19
40+	—		5	15	3	3

discharges, 77%, were based on a Board finding that the subject was no longer dangerous. There was a different pattern of discharge in relation to subjects with longer insanity sentences. Sixty-eight percent of those discharged as no longer mentally ill had sentences of 10 years or more, compared with only 32% of those discharged as no longer dangerous.

There were significant differences between the three groups in relation to their prior involvement in the mental health and criminal justice systems (χ^2 = 24.28, df = 6, P = .0005). As illustrated in Figure 7–1, those subjects whose jurisdiction elapsed and those discharged as no longer dangerous were similar and both were very different from those subjects discharged as no longer mentally ill. This latter group had less experience in the mental health system and more experience with the criminal justice system. These distinctions between the three groups appear to continue after discharge from PSRB jurisdiction.

Table 7–6 depicts the criminal justice contacts for the sample after discharge from PSRB jurisdiction. There was a significant difference between the three discharge types in the mean number of criminal justice contacts after discharge. This difference did not hold up when the number of contacts were corrected for time of follow-up.

To investigate this area in more detail, we first compared the criminal justice contacts of the two discretionary discharge groups and found no significant differences between these two groups. We then combined subjects with discretionary discharges and compared them with those subjects with mandatory discharges. We found that a significantly higher percentage of the combined discretionary discharge group had criminal justice contacts (χ^2 = 5.238, df = 1, P = .0221) and a significantly higher mean number of such contacts, (1.54 versus 0.87) (t = 3.212, df = 250, P = .0015). However, when corrected for follow-up time there were no significant differences between the groups.

Table 7–7 describes the mental health system contacts of discharged subjects. There were clear-cut differences among the three groups. Those whom the Board discharged as no longer mentally ill experienced the fewest hospitalizations and spent significantly less time in the postdischarge period in the hospital and in community and residential treatment.

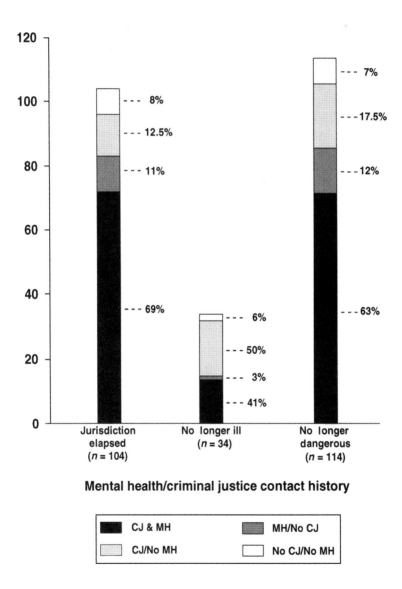

Figure 7–1. Prior mental health (MH) and/or criminal justice (CJ) contacts by discharge type (*N* = 252).

STUDY 3: COMPARISON OF SUBJECTS DISCHARGED FROM HOSPITAL AND THOSE DISCHARGED FROM CONDITIONAL RELEASE

We have previously hypothesized that, barring major differences in subject characteristics, those subjects discharged from the forensic hospital would have higher arrest rates than those discharged from conditional release. We reasoned that those subjects who had achieved a stable involvement in a community placement would continue in this placement after discharge, and that the stability of this mental health treatment setting would reduce future involvement in the criminal justice system. We felt that criminal activity would decrease if the mental illness continued to be treated.

To examine this hypothesis, we compared a subgroup of men who had been placed under PSRB jurisdiction following felony crimes and who had spent the 3 months prior to discharge either in the hospital or on conditional release. We required at least a 3-month period in the hospital or on conditional release prior to discharge to allow those on conditional release time to adjust to

Table 7–6. Criminal justice contacts after discharge

	Jurisdiction elapsed (N = 104)	No longer ill (N = 34)	No longer dangerous (N = 114)
Criminal justice contacts	41 (39%)	20 (59%)	60 (53%)
Mean number of contacts[a]	0.87	1.71	1.49
Average/contacts per year	0.27	0.44	0.37
Type of contact[b]			
Felony	31 (34%)	34 (55%)	72 (41%)
Misdemeanor	60 (66%)	28 (45%)	102 (59%)
Follow-up in years[c]	3.405	4.115	4.167

[a] $F = 5.37$, df = 2,249, $P = .0052$.
[b] $\chi^2 = 6.577$, df = 2, $P = .0373$.
[c] $F = 8.914$, df = 2,245, $P = .0002$.

their community placements. We eliminated women from these comparisons because they had different involvement with the criminal justice system before and after their placement under the jurisdiction of the PSRB (see Chapter 10). We also eliminated misdemeanants because they demonstrated different patterns of hospitalization and conditional release (see Chapter 9). Taking these factors into account we developed a sample of 153 male

Table 7–7. Mental health contacts after discharge

	Jurisdiction elapsed (N =104)	No longer ill (N = 34)	No longer dangerous (N = 114)
Hospital contacts			
Hospital episodes	62 (60%)	18 (53%)	82 (72%)
Mean number of episodes	2.08	1.0	2.26
Range	0–26	0–7	0–19
% of follow-up time in hospital[a]	18	5	13
Community contacts			
Community treatment[b]	62 (60%)	6 (18%)	60 (53%)
% of follow-up time in treatment[c]	28	6	21
Residential services[d]	32 (31%)	0	32 (28%)
% of follow-up time in residential service[e]	9	0	7
Precommitment services[f]	38 (37%)	3 (9%)	38 (33%)
Hospital and community episodes combined			
Number receiving treatment	87 (84%)	24 (74%)	97 (85%)
% of follow-up time receiving service[g]	51	13	37

[a] $F = 3.45$, df = 2,249, $P = .0334$.
[b] $\chi^2 = 18.34$, df = 2, $P = .0001$.
[c] $F = 6.41$, df = 2,249, $P = .0019$.
[d] $\chi^2 = 13.59$, df = 2, $P = .0011$.
[e] $F = 3.13$, df = 2,249, $P = .0456$.
[f] $\chi^2 = 9.53$, df = 2, $P = .0085$.
[g] $F = 13.42$, df = 2,249, $P = .0000$.

subjects, 92 whom the PSRB discharged from the hospital and 61 discharged from conditional release.

Demographically, we found those discharged from the hospital to be significantly younger, with a mean age of 29 compared to 33 for the conditionally released group (t = 2.06, df = 148, P = .0412). We found no significant differences between the groups in relation to diagnosis, marital status, past history of substance abuse, and whether the Board discharged these subjects on a mandatory or discretionary basis.

In addition to spending the last 3 months either in the hospital or on conditional release, the hospitalized group spent significantly more time, on average, in the hospital, 21 months compared to 15 months (t = 2.28, df = 151, P = .0242), and the conditionally released subjects spent significantly more time, on average, in the community, 28 months compared to 1 month (t = 14.86, df = 151, P = .0000). Looking at these findings in another way, the hospitalized group spent 96% of their time under PSRB jurisdiction in the hospital compared to 29% for the conditionally released subjects (t = 21.9, df = 151, P = .0000).

An interesting and unexpected finding demonstrated that those subjects in the conditional release group spent, on average, significantly more time under PSRB jurisdiction, 44 months compared to 23 months for those in the hospitalized group (t = 6.05, df = 151, P = .0000). We found this result despite the fact that there was no significant variation between the groups in the seriousness of the crimes leading to PSRB jurisdiction or in the length of assignment to the PSRB. There also was no significant difference between the two groups in the type of discharge, mandatory versus discretionary.

Mental Health and Criminal Justice System Contacts After Discharge From PSRB Jurisdiction

The critical issue in this study is the question of whether there are differences in adjustment after discharge for those subjects discharged from the hospital compared to those discharged from conditional release. As an overview, Figure 7–2 demonstrates significant differences between these two discharge groups using the outcome variables of mental health and criminal justice system contacts. Fifty-five percent of those discharged from the hospital had both mental health and criminal justice contacts while 59% of those discharged from conditional release had no contact with either system after discharge from PSRB jurisdiction. Look-

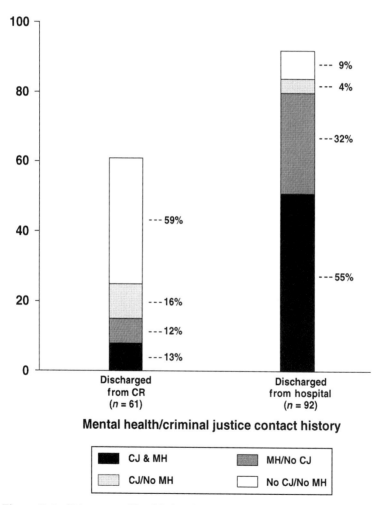

Figure 7–2. Prior mental health (MH) and/or criminal justice (CJ) contacts by discharge from conditional release (CR) and hospital ($N = 153$).

ing at these findings from another perspective, 71% of those discharged from conditional release had no criminal justice contacts in the follow-up period compared to 41% for those discharged from the hospital.

Comparison of Mental Health and Criminal Justice System Contacts Before and After Assignment to PSRB Jurisdiction

The dramatic differences between the two groups in their postdischarge contacts with the mental health and criminal justice systems needs to be compared with the involvement of these subjects in these two systems prior to their assignment to the jurisdiction of the Board.

Mental Health Contacts

Because we did not have consistent community data across the entire study period we compared only the pre-PSRB and postdischarge use of state hospitals for the two groups of subjects. We found no significant differences between the groups in the number of subjects hospitalized or in the mean number of hospitalizations prior to the involvement of subjects with the PSRB.

There were, however, significant differences in the follow-up period. Although there was no difference between the groups in the percentages of those hospitalized on a voluntary basis there were significant differences in involuntary hospitalization. Eighty-six percent of those subjects whom the Board discharged from the hospital were hospitalized involuntarily at some point during the follow-up period compared to only 18% of those subjects the Board discharged from conditional release (χ^2 = 69.69, df = 1, P = .0000). In addition, subjects discharged from the hospital had an average of 1.8 involuntary hospitalizations compared to 0.4 for those discharged from conditional release, (t = 6.02, df = 150, P = .0000). The subjects discharged from the hospital spent an average of 20% of the follow-up period hospitalized involuntarily, significantly more than the 2% for the conditional release group (t =2.94, df = 151, P = .0038).

Criminal Justice Contacts

There were significant differences between the two groups in relation to criminal justice contacts both before and after PSRB jurisdiction as depicted in Table 7–8. Although 89% of both groups had police contacts prior to the PSRB, those discharged from the hospital had significantly more contacts with the criminal justice system in terms of absolute numbers and when corrected by yearly rates.

After PSRB jurisdiction there also were significant differences between the groups. Sixty-three percent of subjects discharged from the hospital had criminal justice system contacts compared with 34% of those subjects discharged from conditional release. In addition, the hospital discharge group had significantly more

Table 7–8. Criminal contacts before and after PSRB jurisdiction ($N = 153$)

Criminal justice data	Discharge from hospital ($N = 92$)	Discharge from conditional release ($N = 61$)
Prior contacts	82 (89%)	54 (89%)
Prior contacts (mean)[a]	5.5	3.7
Average/year[b]	0.6	0.4
Seriousness score	431	406
Type of contacts		
Misdemeanor	176 (34%)	69 (30%)
Felony	336 (66%)	159 (70%)
Post contacts[c]	58 (63%)	21 (34%)
Post contacts (mean)[d]	2.0	0.7
Average/year[e]	0.4	0.2
Seriousness score[f]	459	512
Type of contacts		
Misdemeanor	76 (44%)	23 (59%)
Felony	97 (56%)	16 (41%)

[a] $t = 3.75$, df = 151, $P = .0003$.
[b] $t = 2.32$, df = 149, $P = .0214$.
[c] $\chi^2 = 2.028$, df = 1, $P = .0005$.
[d] $t = 4.71$, df = 151, $P = .0000$.
[e] $t = 3.08$, df = 150, $P = .0025$.
[f] $t = 2.10$, df = 77, $P = .0389$.

criminal justice contacts that remained when we corrected the data for time during follow-up.

Also as demonstrated in Table 7–8, we found no difference in the seriousness of the crimes in the pre-PSRB time period, but we found a significant difference in the average seriousness score of the criminal contacts in the follow-up period. Those discharged from the hospital had arrests for more serious crimes.

Community Mental Health Services After Discharge From PSRB Jurisdiction

We were very interested in the question of whether there were differences between those subjects discharged from the hospital compared with those discharged from conditional release in relation to enrollment in community mental health programs after discharge. We were also interested in whether there was a difference in the time it took for subjects to enter these programs.

Forty-one percent of those discharged from conditional release and 43% of those discharged from the hospital received services from a community mental health program. However, as Table 7–9 demonstrates, there were significant differences in the time it took for those who received services to get into a community program. Sixty percent of those subjects discharged from conditional release entered a community program within 1 month of discharge by the Board, while it took 12 months for 53% of the

Table 7–9.   Time to first community episode

Time to first community contact (months)[a]	Discharge from hospital (N = 40)	Discharge from conditional release (N = 25)
0–1	6 (15%)	15 (60%)
2–12	15 (38%)	5 (20%)
> 12	19 (47%)	5 (20%)
Mean in days[b]	580	267

[a] $\chi^2 = 14.32$, df = 2, $P = .0008$.
[b] $t = 2.08$, df = 63, $P = .0416$.

subjects discharged from the hospital to enter community mental health service. It took hospitalized subjects a mean of 580 days to enter a community program, significantly higher than the 267 days it took for conditionally released subjects to enter community programs.

DISCUSSION

This chapter examined the involvement of insanity acquittees in the mental health and criminal justice systems after discharge from the jurisdiction of the PSRB. How subjects adjust after they are discharged is important from several perspectives. From a mental health services research perspective, it is critical to know as much as possible about this group of individuals because of their demonstrated past heavy use of both mental health and criminal justice system services (see Chapter 3). It is important to establish whether their involvement in the mental health and criminal justice systems after discharge returns to pre-PSRB levels and whether the treatment they received while under the jurisdiction of the Board appears to make a difference in postdischarge adjustment. These areas have important implications for the design of programs to serve similar populations.

There are also implications from the data presented in this chapter for the design of forensic mental health systems. The PSRB operates within a legal framework that potentially could be altered by the Oregon legislature. For example, within the constitutional parameters provided by the United States Supreme Court in *Jones v. U.S.* (10), Oregon could eliminate the defined period of the insanity sentence in favor of a system that has no mandated limit to the length of Board jurisdiction. In this model, discharge would become entirely "discretionary" based on a Board finding that an individual is no longer dangerous and/or mentally ill. As another example, the legislature could expand or contract the jurisdiction of the Board. In 1983 a proposal was placed before the Oregon legislature to have the PSRB manage all mentally ill offenders, including those in the prison. Or, Oregon could adopt the strategy promulgated in Connecticut and limit the Board's authority to the conditional release or discharge of insanity acquittees who are committed to the jurisdiction of the Board following major felonies. Or, in this period of fiscal constraint on government, the legislature might choose to subsume the powers of the PSRB under the state parole board. This latter proposal was recently discussed and rejected in Oregon.

The question of the discharge of insanity acquittees from forensic facilities goes hand in glove with the problem of the prediction of dangerousness (11, 12). The PSRB is making predictions each time it places an insanity acquittee in the community on conditional release, revokes a conditional release, or when it discharges an individual based on a finding that the individual is no longer dangerous. By discharging individuals as no longer dangerous, the PSRB is developing its own history in the area of prediction. This track record is open to scrutiny. Thus there are very important program implications for the follow-up data presented in this chapter and each of the studies presented were designed to attempt to address such policy questions.

The data presented in study 1 of this chapter are generally in line with the data reported from Maryland (5, 6). With an average follow-up time of 53 months, 65% of subjects in our study were hospitalized at least once, 50% had at least one arrest and 40% had both a hospitalization and an arrest. These rates of contact with the mental health and criminal justice systems were clearly influenced by the length of the follow-up period. Those subjects with postdischarge contacts with either system had significantly longer follow-up times in the community. Given the caution pointed out in the Maryland research, where rearrests plateaued at 66% 10 years after discharge, we should expect an increase in the rearrest rate of the subjects in our study.

There also was an apparent difference in the data from Oregon and Maryland in that arrests in Oregon seemed to occur more proximately to discharge, 52% of first arrests in the first year after discharge in this study and 77% in our earlier study (7). These differences between the jurisdictions might well relate to the fact that in the Maryland data, the follow-up period included those subjects discharged from hospital who were placed on conditional release for part of the study period. If the time period on conditional release were added to the Oregon data the length of time to first arrest would increase.

The difference in the Oregon data between the earlier and the current studies could be explained by the fact that the earlier study had a limited data base as compared with the data base used for this chapter. Our results suggest a clear need for more research in this area from other jurisdictions. The differences between our data and those presented from California (8) again are most likely explained by the length of the follow-up period.

Although the percentage of subjects hospitalized in state psychiatric hospitals did not change dramatically when we compared pre- and post-PSRB usage, criminal justice system contacts did change significantly. The numbers of criminal justice contacts decreased significantly from 0.5 to 0.3 contacts per year and there was an overall decrease in felonies and increase in misdemeanors among those subjects who were arrested. In addition, as has been found in relation to other mentally ill populations (13, 14) there was a significant relationship between those who were arrested before and after PSRB jurisdiction.

The decrease in the amount of criminal justice contacts per year following discharge from PSRB is important, but certain cautions must be taken when interpreting these results. Although subjects without post-PSRB criminal justice contacts had an average of 3.81 years of follow-up, subjects with post-PSRB contacts had significantly longer time in follow-up, averaging 5.04 years. Given the differences in the length of the follow-up period, the decrease in the criminal justice contacts might be more apparent than real. The decrease in criminal justice contacts also might relate to an aging population. Further, given the limited follow-up time, rearrests might be further influenced by incarceration or hospitalization, which would result in fewer "opportunities" for new criminal activities. We do not have data on the length of possible incarceration following arrest, and this area awaits further investigation.

Study 2 examined possible relationships between discharge status and subsequent hospitalization and arrest. We know that the Board curtailed its use of discretionary discharge in the last 3 years of the study period. By choosing our sample for study 2 from those discharged between 1981 and 1985, we are able to get a representative view of the use of discretionary discharge before and after these changes and also to examine the question of how well the Board does in relation to the prediction of dangerousness.

Subjects discharged because their jurisdictional time elapsed and those discharged as no longer dangerous resembled each other in relation to past contacts with the mental health and criminal justice systems. For the most part, these subjects also had short insanity sentences.

Subjects discharged as no longer mentally ill were fewer in number, were predominantly serving insanity sentences of 10 years or more, had significantly more prior contact with the criminal justice system and had fewer contacts with the mental health system. This is a very important group of subjects that the Board found were no longer mentally ill, but might be considered dangerous. In discharging these subjects the Board made an important statement about the limits of its jurisdiction. The decision-making process demonstrated here by the PSRB fits closely to the reasoning in the recent U.S. Supreme Court case of *Foucha v. Louisiana* (15).

A central question in study 2 relates to the future behavior of discharged subjects. The Oregon system mandates discharge at the completion of the insanity sentence. The future behavior of subjects discharged at the termination of this sentence can be used as a benchmark for comparison with those discharged on a discretionary basis. The Oregon legislature, on behalf of the citizens of the state, agreed to accept the risk for those subjects discharged on mandatory basis in exchange for a fair system (see Chapter 12). This is true to a lesser extent with discretionary discharges. In this situation, the legislature gave the Board the power to exercise its judgment in deciding whether to discharge an insanity acquittee as no longer mentally ill or no longer dangerous.

Although both groups of subjects discharged on a discretionary basis had significantly more involvement with the criminal justice system when compared with those subjects with mandatory discharges, the differences were not significant when the data were corrected for time in follow-up. Thus, although trends are apparent there are no significant differences in the criminal justice system involvement between subjects discharged on a mandatory basis and those discharged either as no longer mentally ill or no longer dangerous. The postdischarge mental health contacts of subjects discharged as no longer dangerous were very similar to those discharged because PSRB jurisdiction terminated and were significantly different from those discharged as no longer mentally ill. The latter group had the least involvement with the mental health system, both in relation to hospitalization and community treatment.

Thus in discharging a small number of subjects as no longer mentally ill the Board appears to have been able to identify a group of subjects with considerably less experience with the mental health system both before assignment to the Board's jurisdiction and after discharge. In making the determination that these subjects were not mentally ill, the Board was not saying that these subjects were not dangerous. However, because of the lack of significant postdischarge differences in the groups in relation to criminal justice contacts when these contacts were corrected for time we are unable to reach a conclusion regarding the Board's ability to predict dangerousness. Further clarity in this area may come from examining different subgroups in our data. In addition a longer follow-up time period should also help to settle this question.

Study 3 examined the question of whether subjects discharged from conditional release had fewer criminal justice contacts after discharge than those discharged from the hospital. For this study we used a sample of male felons who were discharged either from the hospital or from conditional release. The subjects discharged from the hospital were significantly younger and spent significantly more of their PSRB time in the hospital. Subjects discharged from conditional release spent significantly more of their PSRB time on conditional release.

A key finding in this study was that subjects discharged from conditional release experienced significantly less involvement with the mental health and criminal justice systems after discharge from the Board's jurisdiction when compared with those discharged from the hospital.

This is a dramatic finding in relation to mental health contacts because there were no significant differences between the two discharge groups in relation to mental health contacts prior to PSRB jurisdiction. The criminal justice system differences are less striking because there were significant differences in the groups in relation to criminal justice contacts prior to PSRB jurisdiction. Even though there were no differences in the groups in their involvement with the mental health system prior to PSRB assignment, we cannot attribute the findings in the mental health area after discharge to whether the subject was discharged from the hospital or from conditional release. As we discussed in Chapter 4, time on conditional release and staying on conditional release without revocation could be the most important variables in relation to subsequent adjustment. Conditional release is not easy to achieve in this system and, again referring to Chapter 4, being placed on conditional release and staying there appears to be mediated by mental status.

This discussion brings subject characteristics to the fore in relation to adjustment of insanity acquittees after discharge. It is also worth noting that subjects discharged from the hospital have a significantly higher involuntary commitment rate when compared with those discharged from conditional release. Having more involuntary hospitalizations might point to a lack of insight on the part of these subjects regarding their mental illnesses and their need for treatment (16).

Subject characteristics may also be very important in relation to community mental health services following hospital discharge. Fifty-six percent of those discharged from conditional release were reported in community mental health treatment within 2 months of discharge, compared with 13% of those discharged from the hospital. It took a mean of 580 days for those discharged from the hospital to enter treatment, if they did, compared with 267 days for those subjects discharged from community placement. These data may represent a linkage problem between hospital and community treatment at the time of discharge from PSRB jurisdiction. Alternatively these findings could highlight limited insight on the part of those discharged from the hospital in relation to understanding their need to be in community treatment after discharge from PSRB.

Ultimately this chapter raises more questions than it answers. The findings presented point to the need for focused studies in this area to further explore adjustment after an insanity acquittee is discharged from an insanity sentence. This is a very fruitful area for further research.

REFERENCES

1. Pasewark RA, Seidenzahl D: Opinions concerning the insanity plea and criminality among mental patients. Bull Am Acad Psychiatry Law 7:199–202, 1979
2. Pasewark RA, Pasewark MD: Insanity revised: once more over the cuckoo's nest. Journal of Psychiatry and Law 481–498, 1978
3. Pasewark RA: Insanity plea: a review of the research literature. Journal of Psychiatry and the Law 9:357–402, 1982
4. Steadman HJ, Braff J: Defendants not guilty by reason of insanity, in Mentally Disordered Offenders: Perspectives From Law and Social Science. Edited by Monahan J, Steadman HJ. New York, Plenum, 1983, pp 109–129
5. Spodak MK, Silver SB, Wright CU: Criminality of discharged insanity acquittees: fifteen year experience in Maryland reviewed. Bull Am Acad Psychiatry Law 12:373–382, 1984
6. Silver SB, Cohen MI, Spodak MK: Follow-up after release of insanity acquittees, mentally disordered offenders, and convicted felons. Bull Am Acad Psychiatry Law 17:387–400, 1989
7. Tellefsen C, Cohen MI, Silver SB, et al: Predicting success on conditional release for insanity acquittees: regionalized versus non-regionalized hospital patients. Bull Am Acad Psychiatry Law 20:87–100, 1992
8. Wiederanders MR: Recidivism of disordered offenders who were conditionally vs. unconditionally released. Behavioral Sciences and the Law 10:141–148, 1992
9. Bloom JD, Rogers JL, Manson SM, et al: Lifetime police contacts of discharged Psychiatric Security Review Board clients. Int J Law Psychiatry 8:189–202, 1986
10. 463 US 354 (1983)
11. Bloom JD, Rogers JL: The legal basis of forensic psychiatry: statutorily mandated psychiatric diagnosis. Am J Psychiatry 144:847–853, 1987
12. Monahan J: The Clinical Prediction of Violent Behavior (DHHS Publ No ADM-81-921). Rockville, MD, National Institute of Mental Health, 1981

13. Steadman HJ, Vaderwyst D, Ribner S: Comparing arrest rates of mental patients and criminal offenders. Am J Psychiatry 135:1218–1220, 1978

14. Shore D, Filson RC, Rae DS: Violent crime arrest rates of White House case subjects and matched control subjects. Am J Psychiatry 147:746–750, 1990

15. Foucha v Louisiana, 112 S. Ct. 1780, 1992

16. Schwartz HI, Vingiano W, Perez CB: Autonomy and the right to refuse treatment: patient attitudes after involuntary medication. Hosp Community Psychiatry 39:1049–1054, 1988

Chapter 8

Diagnostic Issues Related to the Insanity Defense

INTRODUCTION

In this chapter, we focus on the relationship between psychiatric diagnosis and the insanity defense. We begin empirically by comparing subjects from the four most prevalent diagnostic groups in our research sample of 758 subjects (see Chapter 3). These four groups comprised 421 subjects (55%) diagnosed with schizophrenia, 75 subjects (10%) with personality disorder, 56 subjects (7%) with mental retardation, and 46 subjects (6%) with bipolar disorder. After presenting data from this comparison, we discuss issues related to the insanity defense and to the management of each of these four diagnostic groups.

COMPARISON OF INSANITY ACQUITTEES WITH SCHIZOPHRENIA, BIPOLAR DISORDER, PERSONALITY DISORDER, OR MENTAL RETARDATION

Assignment to Psychiatric Security Review Board (PSRB)

There was a significant difference in the patterns of commitment of these four diagnostic groups across the five most populous Oregon counties as seen in Table 8–1. The counties with the fourth and fifth largest populations committed fewer subjects with diagnoses of schizophrenia and approximately twice the numbers of subjects with personality disorders or mental retardation.

Demographics

At the time of assignment to PSRB jurisdiction the subjects with bipolar disorder were significantly older, with a mean age of 37, compared to 31 for the subjects with schizophrenia, 30 for those with personality disorders, and 28 for the mental retardation group (ANOVA, $F = 8.093$, df = 3,587, $P = .0000$). As seen in Table 8–2, the bipolar disorder group also contained significantly more women when compared with the other three diagnostic groups.

Although our data on marital status and education are more limited, we found significant differences among the groups in both of these areas (Table 8–2). Seventy-four percent of those subjects with mental retardation, 65% of the subjects with schizophrenia, 54% of subjects with personality disorders, and 30% of the subjects with bipolar disorder had never married.

Significant differences in educational attainment are also presented in Table 8–2. Seventy-nine percent of those with mental retardation had less than a high school education, compared to 56% of those diagnosed with personality disorders, 43% of those with schizophrenia, and 21% of those with bipolar disorder.

Again as presented in Table 8–2, reported substance abuse was

Table 8–1. Assignment to PSRB jurisdiction from the five most populous counties, by diagnosis

County	Schizophrenia	Personality disorder	Mental retardation	Bipolar disorder
Multnomah	129 (74%)	19 (11%)	14 (8%)	13 (7%)
Rate per 100,000	23	3	2	2
Lane	80 (78%)	8 (8%)	7 (7%)	7 (7%)
Rate per 100,000	30	3	3	3
Washington	16 (73%)	1 (4%)	1 (4%)	4 (18%)
Rate per 100,000	6	0.4	0.4	1
Clackamas	16 (55%)	8 (28%)	3 (10%)	2 (7%)
Rate per 100,000	6	3	1	0.8
Marion	39 (55%)	17 (24%)	11 (15%)	4 (6%)
Rate per 100,000	19	8	5	2

Note. $\chi^2 = 27.766$, df = 12, $P = .0060$.

also significantly different among these four diagnostic groups, with the highest reports in the bipolar subjects.

Past Contacts With the Mental Health System

The schizophrenic and bipolar subjects had a significantly greater number of past hospitalizations—a mean of 4 compared with the subjects with personality disorders or mental retardation, with a mean of 2 prior hospitalizations (ANOVA, $F = 3.732$, df = 3,594, $P = .0112$).

The four diagnostic groups spent significantly different amounts of time in the hospital prior to assignment to PSRB jurisdiction (ANOVA, $F = 4.396$, df = 3,594, $P = .0045$). When we examined post-hoc comparisons between the groups, we found

Table 8–2. Demographic comparisons of four diagnostic groups

	Schizophrenia		Personality disorder		Mental retardation		Bipolar disorder	
N	421		75		56		46	
Sex[a]								
Male	373	89%	66	88%	50	89%	29	63%
Female	48	11%	9	12%	6	11%	17	37%
Marital status[b]								
Never married	215	65%	21	54%	36	74%	12	30%
Widowed/divorced	97	29%	13	33%	10	20%	23	58%
Married	20	6%	5	13%	3	6%	5	12%
Education[c]								
< High school degree	63	43%	9	56%	19	79%	3	21%
High school degree	45	31%	4	25%	5	21%	3	21%
> High school degree	37	26%	3	19%	0		8	57%
Substance abuse[d]								
Not reported	326	77%	50	67%	47	84%	30	65%
Reported	95	23%	25	33%	9	16%	16	35%

[a] $\chi^2 = 23.95$, df = 3, $P = .0000$.
[b] $\chi^2 = 23.716$, df = 6, $P = .0006$.
[c] $\chi^2 = 21.426$, df = 6, $P = .0015$.
[d] $\chi^2 = 8.84$, df = 3, $P = .0315$.

that, although the subjects with mental retardation had fewer hospitalizations, they spent an average of 921 days of their life in the state hospital. This was significantly more than the subjects with schizophrenia (average days = 483, $P = .0018$) and personality disorders (average days = 321, $P = .0006$). Although the subjects with bipolar disorder averaged 596 days for lifetime hospitalization, the difference between this average and the 921 days of hospitalization for the subjects with mental retardation did not reach significance.

Past Contacts With the Criminal Justice System

There were no differences in the number of prior criminal contacts between the groups, the rate of criminal contacts per adult year, or the average seriousness of these prior contacts. When we examined the crime leading to PSRB jurisdiction, we found no differences in the overall percentage of felons and misdemeanants in the four groups, and no difference in the average crime seriousness score.

Hospitalization, Conditional Release, and Discharge

At the time of placement under PSRB jurisdiction the judges conditionally released significantly more bipolar subjects, 28% compared with 12% of the schizophrenic subjects, 11% of the mentally retarded subjects, and 8% of subjects with personality disorders ($\chi^2 = 11.63$, df = 3, $P = .0088$).

The mentally retarded subjects spent an average of 27 months in the hospital, significantly more time hospitalized when compared with the schizophrenic subjects (20 months), subjects with personality disorders (18 months), and bipolar subjects (15 months) (ANOVA, F = 3.212, df = 3,594, $P = .0226$). The bipolar subjects spent the least percentage of time under PSRB jurisdiction, or of the time in the study period, in the forensic hospital, 59%. This was significantly less than the 76% for schizophrenic subjects, 78% for subjects with personality disorder, and 83% for subjects with mental retardation (ANOVA, F = 4.639, df = 3,594, $P = .0032$).

Once conditionally released, there were no differences among the diagnostic groups in the number of months spent on conditional release or in the numbers of conditional release episodes that ended in revocation or discharge.

During the study period, the Board discharged 69% of those subjects with personality disorder, compared with 50% of the schizophrenic, bipolar, and mentally retarded subjects ($\chi^2 = 10.29$, df = 3, $P = .0163$). Of those discharged, the Board gave discretionary discharges to 76% of subjects with personality disorders, again compared with about 50% for the other groups ($\chi^2 = 11.03$, df = 3, $P = .0115$). Chapter 5 placed these findings in the context of Board decision making over a 12-year time period.

DISCUSSION

Psychiatric diagnosis is important at several junctures in the criminal justice process that leads from arrest to trial to disposition. This book is predominantly focused on a cohort of insanity acquittees and their subsequent commitment to the jurisdiction of the PSRB. The material presented in this chapter allows us to discuss some issues related to the trial process that leads to a successful insanity defense.

Psychiatric diagnosis is critical to the successful pursuit of an insanity defense (1). We have argued (2) that the insanity defense should be reserved for very seriously mentally ill individuals, primarily those with psychoses for which treatment technologies exist for both hospital and community treatment. A narrowly applied insanity defense fits into our criminal justice system, which emphasizes personal responsibility. Exculpation because of insanity has never been universally tolerated in our society. Its application over the years in very narrow circumstances has permitted the defense to remain viable regardless of the controversy that has surrounded it.

Schizophrenia and bipolar disorder are the major diagnostic entities whose psychopathology most appropriately fit legal definitions of insanity. Both potentially affect an individual's ability to think rationally. Subjects with personality disorders are individuals whose diagnoses raise significant problems with regard to the insanity defense at trial and after trial. Mentally retarded insanity acquittees present different concerns. Each of these diagnostic entities will be discussed separately.

Schizophrenia

Schizophrenia is the most prevalent psychiatric disorder associated with a successful insanity defense, a trend we noted in the first 5 years of PSRB functioning (3) that is now confirmed with this larger sample and in reports from other jurisdictions (4, 5). As the negative effects of deinstitutionalization become more apparent (6, 7), there are reports of large numbers of seriously and chronically mentally ill individuals in the criminal justice system in jails (8–12) and prisons (13). The great majority of these individuals have schizophrenia.

In a previous paper (14), we focused on the mental health and criminal justice system involvement of a sample of 381 insanity acquittees with schizophrenia. The data presented in that paper and in this book confirm that most subjects with schizophrenia have extensive experience with the mental health and criminal justice systems prior to their assignment to PSRB jurisdiction and after discharge.

Bipolar Disorder

Bipolar subjects were clearly different from others in the sample in a number of ways. The bipolar subjects were significantly older and included significantly more women—37% compared with an average of approximately 11% for the other groups. In addition, more bipolar subjects had married; only 30% of these bipolar subjects had never married, compared with 65% of those with schizophrenia. We also found that bipolar subjects had the highest reported substance abuse of the four groups. As we discussed in Chapter 3, we believe that the amount of substance abuse is underreported for this sample as a whole.

Both the judges and the PSRB managed the bipolar subjects differently from the other diagnostic subgroups. The judges and the PSRB conditionally released significantly more bipolar subjects compared with other diagnostic groups. Overall, bipolar subjects spent significantly less time in the hospital compared with the other three groups. These were not unexpected differences given the natural history of this serious mental illness.

Mental Retardation

Our research was not designed to emphasize the problems of mentally retarded people in the criminal justice system. However, even limited consideration leads to questions about the relationship of mentally retarded individuals to criminal law in general (15, 16) and to the insanity defense in particular (17). Estimates of the prevalence of mentally retarded insanity acquittees are summarized in an article by Petrilla (18) and range from 0.19% in a report in California to 8.5% in a report from Virginia.

Assuming a relatively stable prevalence of mentally retarded individuals across the country, these differences may reflect several issues. They may represent diagnostic differences in the various studies. The differences may be related to jurisdictional variations in how the insanity defense is utilized for mentally retarded offenders. They also may reflect different numbers of mentally retarded people at risk for entering the criminal justice system. One state may still care for large numbers of mentally retarded individuals in large state facilities, while another may have moved in the direction of deinstitutionalization. Alternatively, community services for retarded citizens may be marginal, adequate, or excellent. This is an area for further research.

Further questions concern the problems of providing adequate programs for mentally retarded individuals once they have raised a successful insanity defense. Programs should emphasize education and habilitation in an effort to manage mentally retarded offenders appropriately (19).

In the data presented in this chapter, we report a prevalence rate of 7% of the sample who are diagnosed with mental retardation. Although, as we mentioned, we did not focus our research on this population, several points are clear from the data presented in this chapter. As one might expect, individuals with mental retardation were the least frequently married of all the groups in our comparison study and had the lowest levels of educational attainment. They also demonstrated the lowest levels of comorbid substance abuse among the four groups in the comparison study. Although these subjects had half as many previous hospitalizations as did schizophrenic and bipolar subjects, hospitalized mentally retarded subjects spent an average of 2.5 years in the hospital prior to their assignment to PSRB jurisdiction.

While under PSRB jurisdiction, mentally retarded subjects spent significantly more time hospitalized compared with the other three groups, both in terms of actual months and in terms of the percentage of their PSRB time or of the study period. These findings point to a need for further study of this population, which would lead to a better understanding of their characteristics and a more effective focus on their treatment needs. There is nothing inherent in the PSRB model that could not be adapted to the specific needs of mentally retarded people in a manner similar to what we have defined for chronically mentally ill individuals.

Personality Disorder

Individuals with nonpsychotic, nonorganic disorders have posed significant problems in relation to the administration of the insanity defense, both at the trial and at disposition. The most recent wave of insanity defense reforms in the United States followed the trial of John Hinckley, Jr., and were aimed primarily at narrowing the scope of the insanity defense. There was general interest in developing statutory changes that would prevent what might be perceived as inappropriate use of the insanity defense by individuals who are not severely mentally ill. This discussion was partly aimed at persons whose sole psychiatric diagnosis was that of personality disorder. This focus was evident either directly or indirectly in the various proposals put forth at that time. For example, the American Psychiatric Association advocated for the elimination of the volitional prong of the American Law Institute insanity test (20). This proposal was indirectly aimed at individuals with personality disorder. Others proposed restricting insanity defenses for crimes associated with behavioral disorders, such as compulsive gambling (21).

Oregon joined the national trend on this issue in the legislative session that took place immediately after the Hinckley verdict. The impetus for change in Oregon came primarily from forensic hospital psychiatrists, who supported a proposal to bar the insanity defense for those whose only diagnosis was personality disorder. The legislature supported this proposal. The language of the insanity defense was amended to prohibit an insanity defense for individuals whose diagnosis consisted of "any abnormality constituting solely a personality disorder" (22).

As we have reported here, those with personality disorders represent 10% of our sample of 758 subjects. This appears to be high when compared with other jurisdictions. A recent article from Connecticut (23) compared psychiatric diagnosis of insanity acquittees in Connecticut with those from three other jurisdictions including Oregon. They found that Connecticut and Oregon reported significantly higher rates of individuals with personality disorder when compared to Illinois and, to a lesser extent, to New York. Another recent article describing insanity defense reform in California (5) reported rates of personality disorder insanity acquittees at 3.1% before and 1.1% after a 1982 reform in California statutes.

We have also reported differential commitment rates by diagnosis in Oregon's most populous counties. The fifth most populous county committed more than twice the number of subjects with personality disorders than did the other four most populous counties. This finding illustrates the critical roles of the trial court, the prosecutor, and the defense attorney in determining who achieves an insanity verdict. In contrast to the rigor that characterizes the PSRB and its role in the management and care of insanity acquittees, Oregon is a state with a laissez-faire approach to the insanity defense prior to the rendering of an insanity verdict (24). There are no court clinics in Oregon. There is no standardized approach for qualifying expert witnesses. Many evaluations are done in the private sector involving a large number of psychiatrists and psychologists, and only a small percentage of pretrial evaluations are done at the forensic unit of the Oregon State Hospital. Given this situation and the fact that judges and prosecutors may differ in how they understand the insanity defense and in how they approach their responsibilities in this area, it should not be surprising that Oregon had what appears to be a larger percentage of individuals with personality disorder within its population of insanity acquittees. In addition, as illustrated in this book, Oregon maintains tight controls over insanity acquittees who are committed to the PSRB. Prosecutors generally might prefer to have an individual under the jurisdiction of the Board, because the individual is likely to spend more time in an institution or under community supervision than they would under the corrections system, with its limitations on bed space and parole supervision.

Substance abuse was reported in 33% of the subjects with personality disorders. The Epidemiologic Catchment Area studies (25) reported comorbidity between substance abuse and antisocial personality disorder at 84%. Again, we attribute the finding of 33% comorbidity in this sample to underreporting and to the fact that our sample represents individuals with personality disorders with mixed features and thus is not restricted to those who are purely antisocial.

Once under PSRB jurisdiction, the data from our comparison study demonstrate that subjects with personality disorders are handled differently from subjects in the three other diagnostic groups. During the study period, the Board discharged significantly more subjects with personality disorders, especially under the Board's discretionary authority to grant early discharges. These findings are largely explained in Chapter 5 and reflect the heavy use of discretionary discharge in the first 3 years of the functioning of the PSRB. It has been reported to us by individuals who worked with the Board during that period that these discharge decisions were a means of making a point to the trial courts and to county prosecutors that personality disorder insanity acquittees were not "mentally ill" and hence were not appropriate individuals for an insanity verdict. Members of the Board thought that if insanity acquittees with personality disorders were discharged, the judges and prosecutors would look more carefully at diagnostic issues at trial and the prosecutors would contest these cases more strenuously. As is evident from our discussion in Chapter 5, the numbers of discretionary discharges dropped dramatically in subsequent years, and individuals with personality disorder are now retained in the system equally as long as those with schizophrenia (26).

In an earlier paper (27), we reconstructed the trial process of 316 insanity acquittees who were placed under PSRB jurisdiction from 1978 to 1981. Eighty-six percent of these cases involved an uncontested hearing in which judge, prosecutor, and defense attorney all agreed to an insanity verdict. Diagnosis did play a significant role in whether a case was contested rather than conceded. Thirty percent of the group with personality disorders, compared to 12% of the group with schizophrenia, had a contested hearing. This still left some 70% of those with personality disorders with uncontested verdicts.

In summary, the overall picture of how individuals with personality disorders are handled in Oregon is complicated by many factors. Attempts to bar them from the system at the front door have not been totally successful. Early discharge by the Board, as a message to prosecutors and judges, has given way to the management stance documented in this book, in which jurisdiction is retained within the system and they are maintained in the system in a manner more closely paralleling the management of the schizophrenic subjects. New avenues for exploration might be the development in Oregon of a more tightly organized system of court clinic evaluation and/or the development of standards for the appointment of experts for pretrial evaluation.

CONCLUSION

This chapter has given us the opportunity to explore wide-ranging issues regarding diagnostic factors in the insanity defense system. It is important to reiterate that the largest problem facing the PSRB is the management and treatment of chronic schizophrenia. It is also essential that we not lose sight of the other diagnostic groups under the jurisdiction of the Board and the challenges that they bring to those charged with their management.

Public policymakers need to be familiar with the natural course of these conditions before attempting to design programs for these individuals. For example, bipolar disorder is a chronic mental illness most often characterized by exacerbations and remissions. It is an illness that fits the hospitalization and community support models described throughout this book. Without engaging in debate about whether mental retardation fits into the disease model of the insanity defense, this condition can be managed under a Review Board system with an emphasis on the special needs of this population.

Finally, there is the multifaceted problem of the individuals with personality disorders—that is, whether they should be "allowed" to raise an insanity defense, and once it is successfully raised, how they should they be managed. Again, different models of care need to be developed for this group, most likely along the lines of programs that emphasize cognitive restructuring as developed for the treatment of people with substance abuse problems or for individuals with antisocial personality disorders (28). There is a great need for more program development in this area—programs that certainly could benefit a large number of mentally ill offenders.

REFERENCES

1. Steadman HJ, Keitner L, Braff J, et al: Factors associated with a successful insanity plea. Am J Psychiatry 140:401–405, 1983
2. Bloom JD, Bradford J, Kofoed L: An overview of psychiatric treatment approaches to three offender groups. Hosp Community Psychiatry 39:151–158, 1988
3. Rogers JL, Bloom JD, Manson SM: Oregon's new insanity defense system: a review of the first five years, 1978–1982. Bull Am Acad Psychiatry Law 12:383–402, 1984
4. Petrilla J: The insanity defense and other mental health dispositions in Missouri. Int J Law Psychiatry 5:81–101, 1982
5. McGreevy MA, Steadman HJ, Callahan LA: The negligible effects of California's 1982 reform of the insanity defense test. Am J Psychiatry 148:744–750, 1991
6. Lamb HR: What did we really expect from deinstitutionalization? Hosp Community Psychiatry 32:105–109, 1981
7. Minkoff K: Beyond deinstitutionalization: A new ideology for the post institutional era. Hosp Community Psychiatry 38:945–950, 1987
8. Lamb HR, Grant R: The mentally ill in an urban county jail. Arch Gen Psychiatry 39:17–22, 1982

9. Steadman HJ, McCarthy DW, Morrissey JP: The Mentally Ill in Jail. New York, Guilford, 1989

10. Teplin LA: The prevalence of severe mental disorder among male urban jail detainees: comparison with the epidemiologic catchment area program. Am J Public Health 80:663–669, 1990

11. Palermo GB, Smith MB, Liska FJ: Jails versus mental hospitals: a social dilemma. International Journal of Offender Therapy and Comparative Criminology 35:97–107, 1991

12. Arvanites TM: A comparison of civil patients and incompetent defendants: pre- and post-deinstitutionalization. Bull Am Acad Psychiatry Law 18:393–403, 1990

13. Jamelka R, Trupin E, Chiles JA: The mentally ill in prisons: a review. Hosp Community Psychiatry 40:481–491, 1989

14. Bloom JD, Williams MH, Bigelow DA: The involvement of schizophrenic insanity acquittees in the mental health and criminal justice systems. Psychiatr Clin North Am 15:591–604, 1992

15. Ellis JW, Luckasson RA: Mentally retarded criminal defendants. George Washington Law Review 53:414–493, 1985

16. Hodgins S: Mental disorder, intellectual deficiency and crime. Arch Gen Psychiatry 49:476–483, 1992

17. Fitch LW: Mental retardation and criminal responsibility, in The Criminal Justice System and Mental Retardation. Edited by Conley RW, Luckasson RA, Bouthilet GN, et al. Baltimore, MD, Paul H Brookes Publishing, 1992, pp 121–136

18. Petrilla RC: Defendants with mental retardation in the forensic services system, in The Criminal Justice System and Mental Retardation. Edited by Conley RW, Luckasson RA, Bouthilet GN, et al. Baltimore, MD, Paul H Brookes Publishing, 1992, pp 79–96

19. Wood HR, White DL: A model for habilitation and prevention for offenders with mental retardation: the Lancaster County (PA) Office of Special Offender Services, in The Criminal Justice System and Mental Retardation. Edited by Conley RW, Luckasson RA, Bouthilet GN, et al. Baltimore, MD, Paul H Brookes Publishing, 1992, pp 153–165

20. Insanity Defense Work Group: American Psychiatric Association statement on the insanity defense. Am J Psychiatry 140:681–688, 1983

21. Rachlin S, Halpern AL, Portnow SL: The volitional rule, personality disorders, and the insanity defense. Psychiatric Annals 14:139–147, 1984

22. Oregon Revised Statutes, §161.295

23. Zonana HV, Wells JA, Getz MA, et al: Part I: the NGRI registry; initial analyses of data collected on Connecticut insanity acquittees. Bull Am Acad Psychiatry Law 18:115–128, 1990

24. Reichlin SM, Bloom JD, Williams MH: Assessments of mental health examination reports. Paper presented at the annual meeting of the American Academy of Psychiatry and the Law, San Diego, CA, October 1990

25. Reiger DA, Farmer ME, Rae DS, et al: Comorbidity of mental disorders with alcohol and other drug abuse. JAMA 264:2511–2518, 1990

26. Reichlin SM, Bloom JD, Williams MH: Post-Hinckley insanity reform in Oregon. Bull Am Acad Psychiatry Law 18:405–413, 1990

27. Rogers JL, Bloom JD, Manson SM: Insanity defenses: contested or conceded. Am J Psychiatry 141:885–888, 1984

28. Reid WR: The antisocial personality: a review. Hosp Community Psychiatry 36:831–837, 1985

Chapter 9

Misdemeanants and the Psychiatric Security Review Board

I have been seriously mentally ill since 1982. Through these years of many times being sick, confused, lost, despondent and afraid, there are few times I felt these feelings more than when I was handcuffed, driven in the caged back end of a squad car and taken to sit in a small cell for days. . . . You shouldn't have to become a part of the criminal justice system to get mental health care in America. (1)

In this chapter, we describe misdemeanants under the jurisdiction of the Psychiatric Security Review Board (PSRB). This focus provides us with the opportunity to highlight the controversial question of the criminalization of mentally ill people (2). The issue of criminalization is a difficult and controversial area that has received much attention in the literature. There is debate about whether criminalization has actually taken place (3) and whether what is described as criminalization represents in actuality more mental patients in jails (4) or more criminals in mental hospitals (5). We have been convinced—from our clinical activities, our previous case studies of insanity acquittees (6), our survey of family members of the Oregon Alliance for the Mentally Ill (7), the material presented in this book, and prior work in the area of civil commitment (8)—that criminalization of mentally ill people has taken place and continues to take place in various ways in Oregon.

One type of criminalization may bring individuals to the jurisdiction of the PSRB. We have heard, on an anecdotal basis, from many family members of mentally ill people in Oregon about their attempts to have criminal charges brought against their mentally ill relatives in order to have them committed to the jurisdiction of the PSRB. Commitment to the jurisdiction of the PSRB has been portrayed to us as a means of obtaining the treatment that their relatives would not willingly accept on a voluntary basis and had not received under Oregon's civil commitment laws.

From a national perspective, criminalization is frequently linked to the changes in civil commitment law that have occurred over the past two decades (9, 10). In this model, the hypothesis is that fewer mentally ill individuals are being civilly committed. This reduction has resulted from changes in civil commitment statutes, which have placed increased emphasis on due process protection and on a narrowing of the definition of mental illness for commitment purposes to rely heavily on current dangerousness (11). In this conceptual model, the stricter the commitment law, the more individuals will be excluded from this process. Once excluded from civil commitment and from the possibility of asylum, these individuals are subject to further social breakdown in the form of poor community care, increased substance abuse, and (for some) the extreme condition of homelessness (12). Placed in a more vulnerable status, these individuals then become candidates for other forms of social control, such as entry into the criminal justice system.

It is difficult to test hypotheses about criminalization; commitment laws will be applied differently, and mental health resources will be more or less available both within (13) and across jurisdictions. As a result, the numbers of those at risk for entry into the criminal justice system should vary from location to location. Hence, criminalization may be reported in a particular study and not in others. In addition, the relationship between the mental health and criminal justice systems is in a constant state of change so that at one time criminalization is apparent in a jurisdiction but may not be at another time (14).

These relationships may be altered by major changes in civil commitment statutes that make diversion into the criminal justice system more or less attractive (15, 16), or the relationships may change as a result of more minor system changes unrelated to changes in the law. For example, several years ago in Portland, Oregon, county government changed their policies related to the transportation of mentally ill patients to the local state hospital and designated the police as the responsible agents for transport. As a result of this change in procedure, the police arrested and booked more mentally ill individuals into the county jail on minor criminal charges rather than institute a police hold for mental illness and drive the 17 miles to the state hospital.

This change in the system lasted but a short time, but the example illustrates the effects of relatively minor policy changes on the issue of criminalization. It is crucial to understand that the police have a great deal of latitude in relation to minor crimes, and a person's particular behavior might equally constitute "dangerous" behavior under the civil commitment law or a misdemeanor crime. The police do the initial screening and must make a choice regarding which statutory mechanisms they choose to invoke.

In this chapter, we focus on these issues as we describe misdemeanants committed to the jurisdiction of the PSRB. The original PSRB legislation passed in 1977 included all individuals who successfully raised an insanity defense following either a felony or misdemeanor crime and whom the trial court determined were dangerous. The 1981 Oregon Legislative Assembly amended the statutes to limit assignment of insanity acquittees to the PSRB to those cases in which "the court finds that the person would have been guilty of a felony, or of a misdemeanor during a criminal episode in the course of which the person caused physical injury or risk of physical injury to another" (17). For cases involving "a misdemeanor during a criminal episode in the course of which the person did not cause physical injury or risk of physical injury to another," the legislature modified the statute to require the court to proceed under the state's civil commitment procedures (18).

We focus here on those individuals assigned to the jurisdiction of the PSRB as a result of charges for misdemeanor crimes and compare these subjects with those acquittees assigned as a result of charges for felony crimes. We examine demographics, prior involvement in the mental health and criminal justice systems, placement while under the Board's jurisdiction, and subsequent involvement in the criminal justice and mental health systems for those discharged.

COMPARISON OF MISDEMEANANTS AND FELONS UNDER PSRB JURISDICTION

We have classified subjects into the "misdemeanant" and "felon" categories based on the most serious crime charged against them according to the seriousness scale described in Chapter 3. Since its inception in 1978, 24% of all individuals assigned to the jurisdiction of the PSRB have been charged only with misdemeanor crimes. Of the 758 subjects who make up the core sample for this book, 204 (27%) were charged only with misdemeanor offenses, and 554 (73%) had a felony crime as their most serious charge.

Jurisdictional Issues

There were differences in the rates of commitment of misdemeanants to the PSRB by county courts in Oregon's five most populous counties. Together, these five counties account for 66% of the study sample. As presented in Table 9–1, there were significant differences in the various percentages of misdemeanants committed from these counties. Lane, Washington, and Marion counties committed a higher percentage of misdemeanants when compared with the other counties.

Table 9–1. Assignment to the PSRB by county

County	Misdemeanant group		Felon group	
	Frequency	%	Frequency	%
Multnomah[a]	45	21	173	79
Rate per 100,000	8		31	
Lane	47	35	88	65
Rate per 100,000	17		33	
Washington	10	33	20	67
Rate per 100,000	4		7	
Clackamas	8	22	29	78
Rate per 100,000	3		12	
Marion	26	31	57	69
Rate per 100,000	12		27	

[a] $\chi^2 = 10.585$, df = 4, $P = .0316$.

Demographics

The misdemeanant group was 18% female, a significantly higher percentage than the felon group, which was 12% female (χ^2 = 4.00, df = 1, P = .0454). We compared subjects who were never married, married, and those no longer married (widowed, divorced or separated). Significantly, more subjects in the misdemeanant group were married or had been married in the past (χ^2 = 8.57, df = 2, P = .0138). There were no significant differences between the groups in education, age at the time of assignment to PSRB jurisdiction, or diagnosis.

Prior Experience With the Criminal Justice System

We found few differences in subjects' contacts with the criminal justice system prior to assignment to PSRB jurisdiction. In fact, the majority of both groups had prior criminal contacts—80% of the misdemeanant group and 76% of the felon group. The misdemeanant group had an average of 4.4 prior criminal contacts, or 0.52 contacts per adult year. The felon group was very similar, with an average of 4.7 prior criminal contacts and 0.48 contacts per adult year.

Table 9–2 presents these prior contacts for the two groups. As seen in this table, the majority of the prior contacts for the misdemeanant group were for misdemeanor offenses (62%), whereas for the felon group, the prior contacts were evenly divided between felony and misdemeanor offenses. This pattern was significantly different (χ^2 = 29.26, df = 1, P = .0000).

Prior Experience With the State Mental Health System

Eighty percent of the misdemeanants and 76% of the felony subjects had at least one prior psychiatric hospitalization. However, there was a significant difference in the number of prior hospitalizations. The misdemeanant group averaged 3.7 prior hospitalizations, whereas the felon group averaged 2.9 prior hospital episodes (t = 2.3, df = 756, P = .0215). For both groups, most of these hospital episodes were involuntary, with 72% of the misdemeanant group and 70% of the felon group experiencing at least one involuntary episode.

To examine prior community data, we restricted our sample to those individuals assigned to the jurisdiction of the PSRB between 1983 and the end of the study period in 1986 and examined service utilization in the 2 years prior to the PSRB (see Chapter 3). For this reduced sample of 302 subjects, we found significant

Table 9–2.   Criminal justice contacts prior to the PSRB

Crime category	Misdemeanant group (n = 661)		Felon group (n = 1,822)	
	Frequency	%	Frequency	%
Felony crimes	252	38	918	50
Assault	51	8	141	8
Burglary	34	5	175	10
Theft	31	5	93	5
Drug offenses	29	4	112	6
Criminal mischief	24	4	46	3
Escape/failure to appear in court	17	3	80	4
Unauthorized use of auto	16	2	61	3
Robbery	13	2	72	4
Arson	8	1	35	2
Sexual assault	6	1	31	2
Driving offenses	5	1	18	1
Kidnapping	3	< 1	7	< 1
Murder	3	< 1	2	< 1
Attempted homicide	1	< 1	4	< 1
Weapons offenses	1	< 1	2	< 1
Other felony	10	2	39	2
Misdemeanor crimes	409	62	904	50
Theft	114	17	270	15
Menacing/harassment	61	9	123	7
Trespass	60	9	111	6
Driving offenses	54	8	146	8
Resisting arrest	43	7	85	5
Criminal mischief	22	3	37	2
Sexual offenses	22	3	30	2
Escape/failure to appear in court	15	2	37	2
Weapons offenses	8	1	37	2
Arson	4	1	4	< 1
Other misdemeanor	6	1	24	1

differences between the groups in their involvement with the mental health system. Eighty-five percent of the misdemeanants and 71% of the felons received some type of community mental health service in the 2 years prior to assignment to the PSRB (χ^2 = 6.41, df = 1, P = .0114). The misdemeanant subjects spent an average of 33% of this 2-year period enrolled in some type of community services, compared with 24% for the felon group (t = 2.07, df = 300, P = .0395).

We examined the nature of these community services more closely and found that the majority of the services received were for general outpatient treatment services. Sixty-one percent of the misdemeanant group and 49% of the felon subjects received these services in the 2 years prior to assignment to the PSRB. In addition, a significantly larger proportion of the misdemeanant group received precommitment services during this 2-year period—45% of the misdemeanant group compared with 30% of the felon group (χ^2 = 5.84, df = 1, P = .0156). This means that the misdemeanant subjects were more frequently involved in the precommitment stage of the Oregon civil commitment system (19). Only about 10% of both groups received residential services.

When we combined both hospital and community mental health experience for this reduced sample, we found that 93% of the misdemeanant group and 87% of the felon group were involved with state mental health services in the 2 years prior to assignment to PSRB jurisdiction.

Combined Prior Experience With Mental Health and Criminal Justice Systems

Figure 9–1 combines the past psychiatric hospitalization and criminal justice data for all misdemeanant and felon subjects. We found no significant differences between the groups, with the majority of subjects in both groups having had past involvement in both systems.

Misdemeanant and Felon Subjects Under PSRB Jurisdiction

In Chapter 4, we discussed the hospitalization and conditional release of insanity acquittees while under the jurisdiction of the

PSRB. We described the process by which the trial court judge made the initial placement of an individual committed to the jurisdiction of the Board, either to the hospital or on a conditional

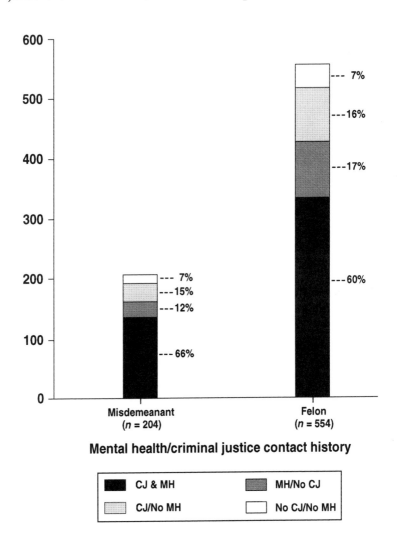

Figure 9–1. Prior mental health (MH) and/or criminal justice (CJ) contacts by misdemeanant or felon subjects.

release to a community mental health treatment program. Judges placed a significantly higher percentage of misdemeanants than of felons on conditional release. However, once the subjects were hospitalized, there was a significant difference in the opposite direction. Of those subjects initially hospitalized by the judges, the Board conditionally released a significantly smaller percentage of misdemeanants as compared with felon subjects.

Between the judges and the Board, 42% of the misdemeanant group and 53% of the felon group had some conditional release time during the study. Of these, the misdemeanant subjects experienced a significantly lower percentage of revocations of their conditional release. Thirty percent of misdemeanants had a revocation of conditional release, compared with 53% of the felony subjects ($\chi^2 = 13.69$, df = 1, $P = .0002$).

For the entire sample, we compared the percentage of PSRB time spent in the hospital versus time on conditional release and found no difference between the misdemeanant and felon groups. The misdemeanant group spent an average of 70% of their jurisdiction time in the hospital, versus 68% for the felon group. Thus, the varying rates of conditional release by the judges and the Board appear to balance out in terms of overall time spent on conditional release.

Of the 86 subjects in the misdemeanant group with some conditional release time, 84% had only one conditional release episode. Of the 295 subjects in the felon group with some conditional release time, only 68% had a single conditional release episode. This difference is explained by the fact that the felon group had a considerably greater length of time under the Board's jurisdiction.

Discharge From Jurisdiction

As detailed in Chapter 7, when the insanity sentence elapses, the Board is required to discharge the acquittee. The Board also is required to discharge an individual who is found to be no longer mentally ill and/or no longer dangerous. As we mentioned earlier, we have called these discretionary discharges. The Board discharged 89% of the misdemeanants during the study period compared to 44% of the felon group ($\chi^2 = 123.56$, df = 1, $P =$

.0000). Not surprisingly, given the disparity between the length of PSRB jurisdiction for misdemeanants and felons, there were significantly more mandatory discharges within the misdemeanant group than within the felon group. When we exclude discharges as a result of natural death, suicide, or court order and then compare the mandatory and discretionary discharges, 70% of the misdemeanant group and 21% of the felon group had mandatory discharges (χ^2 = 93.60, df = 1, P = .0000).

There was a significant difference between the groups in the two major types of discretionary discharges. For the misdemeanants, 88% of these discretionary discharges were as a result of a Board finding that the individual was no longer dangerous. This differs significantly from the 74% for the felon group (χ^2 = 4.94, df = 1, P = .0263).

Misdemeanant and Felon Samples Following Discharge From PSRB Jurisdiction

To compare involvement in the criminal justice and mental health systems following discharge from the PSRB, we selected a subsample of subjects whom the Board discharged between 1981 and 1985. This sample consisted of 102 misdemeanant subjects and 159 felon subjects. We selected this sample in order to have subjects with at least 1 year of community mental health follow-up.

Criminal Justice System Involvement Following Discharge From PSRB Jurisdiction

The misdemeanant and felon groups did not differ significantly in the number of criminal contacts or the rate of contacts per year following discharge from PSRB jurisdiction. The misdemeanant group had an average of 1.3 contacts (0.34 contacts per year), and the felon group had an average of 1.21 contacts (0.35 contacts per year). There was also no difference in the seriousness scores of these contacts, which averaged 501 for the misdemeanant group and 489 for the felon group.

Table 9–3 presents these criminal contacts in the follow-up period. As in the time period before PSRB jurisdiction, there was a statistically significant difference between the groups in the proportions of misdemeanors and felonies in each group. After discharge from PSRB jurisdiction, the misdemeanants' involvement with the criminal justice system was primarily for misdemeanor charges, whereas the contacts of the felony subjects were evenly divided between misdemeanors and felonies ($\chi^2 = 11.72$, df = 1, $P = .0006$).

Table 9–3. Criminal justice contacts following the PSRB (subjects discharged 1981–1985)

Crime category	Misdemeanant group ($n = 135$)		Felon group ($n = 199$)	
	Frequency	%	Frequency	%
Felony crimes	43	32	101	51
Burglary	8	6	27	14
Assault	7	5	11	6
Criminal mischief	5	4	15	8
Unauthorized use of motor vehicle	5	4	9	5
Robbery	5	4	4	2
Escape/failure to appear in court	4	3	13	7
Sexual assault	4	3	4	2
Theft	2	1	10	5
Arson	1	1	2	1
Driving offenses	1	1		
Drug offenses			4	2
Kidnapping			1	1
Other felony	1	1	1	1
Misdemeanor crimes	92	68	98	49
Menacing/harassment	23	17	17	9
Theft	22	16	39	20
Trespass	13	10	15	8
Driving offenses	13	10	8	4
Resisting arrest	6	4	3	2
Sexual offenses	5	4	5	3
Escape/failure to appear in court	4	3	3	2
Weapons offenses	3	2	5	3
Criminal mischief	2	1	3	2
Other misdemeanor	1	1		

Mental Health System Involvement Following
Discharge From PSRB Jurisdiction

We compared the utilization of both community and hospital mental health services following discharge from the PSRB for this same reduced sample of 261 individuals discharged between 1981 and 1985. As depicted in Table 9–4, both groups had extensive involvement with the mental health system after discharge from the PSRB. Although this is not statistically significant, the misdemeanant subjects had more involvement with both hospitalization and community mental health services after discharge from the Board's jurisdiction. When these services are combined, the differences do reach significance for both the number of contacts with the mental health system and the percentage of time in the postdischarge period that a subject was either hospitalized or registered as an active client in a community mental health program.

Table 9–4.   Mental health contacts following the PSRB (subjects discharged 1981–1985)

	Misdemeanant group (N = 102)		Felon group (N = 159)	
	Frequency	**%**	**Frequency**	**%**
Hospitalizations				
Number with episode	74	72	94	59
Mean number	2.48		1.70	
Community services				
Number with episode	76	74	100	63
Total mental health services				
Number with episode[a]	91	89	123	77
Percentage of time registered for service[b]		48		33

[a] $\chi^2 = 5.917$, df = 1, $P = .0150$.
[b] $t = 2.991$, df = 259, $P = .0031$.

DISCUSSION

Has there been criminalization of the misdemeanants in this sample? It is difficult to answer this question directly, because we do not have information about the exact nature of the criminal justice contacts that lead to PSRB jurisdiction. However, without knowing the details of the behaviors that led to the criminal charges, there certainly are important differences that separate the misdemeanants and felons in this sample. These differences raise concerns about the interrelationships between the mental health and criminal justice systems in relation to these misdemeanants. Differences that raise these concerns are as follows:

1. Misdemeanants are committed to the jurisdiction of the PSRB at different rates from the five most populous counties. This finding illustrates intrajurisdictional differences in the commitment of misdemeanants to the PSRB. We reported similar findings across Oregon's counties in relation to civil commitment (13). We have not determined whether counties that use more civil commitment in turn use the PSRB mechanism less.
2. Although the groups shared similar numbers of criminal justice system contacts before and after PSRB jurisdiction, in both time periods they demonstrated significantly different patterns of these criminal contacts. The criminal contacts of the misdemeanants, both before and after PSRB jurisdiction, tended to be misdemeanors, whereas those of the felony subjects were more evenly divided between misdemeanors and felonies. It is important to note that there is also a fair amount of crossover between misdemeanants and felons in terms of criminal contacts both before and after the PSRB. However, there was a sizable group of misdemeanants who did not cross over and whose lifetime criminal contacts are in the misdemeanor range.
3. Both groups had extensive prior experience with the mental health system, both on a lifetime basis and in the 2 years prior to commitment to the PSRB. The past hospitalizations for both groups were predominantly involuntary. However, the misdemeanant subjects had significantly more prior hospitaliza-

tions, and significantly more misdemeanants had contact with the community mental health system in the 2 years prior to their assignment to the jurisdiction of the Board. Further, the misdemeanant subjects received significantly more pre-commitment services in the 2 years prior to the PSRB. This information points to the clear involvement of the misdemeanant population in the civil commitment process in the time period preceding their commitment to the jurisdiction of the Board. How many of these assignments to the jurisdiction of the Board actually represent an alternative to the civil commitment system is unknown. This is an important area that needs empirical investigation.

These differences hold up after discharge from PSRB jurisdiction. Again, both groups had extensive involvement with the mental health system after discharge. However, significantly more misdemeanant subjects had such contacts.

4. Finally, the discharge pattern for the two groups is significantly different in relation to discretionary discharges ordered by the Board. For subjects with discretionary discharges, the Board discharged 88% of the misdemeanant subjects as no longer dangerous, compared with 74% of the felon group. In this particular area and with the crimes that brought these individuals under the jurisdiction of the Board, it is possible that the Board may be applying more of a civil commitment standard for release, based more on current dangerousness than on the presence of chronic mental illness.

Aside from the issue of criminalization, there is a question of whether misdemeanants who have successfully asserted an insanity defense should be assigned to the jurisdiction of the PSRB, or whether they should be diverted to the civil commitment system. What may be gained and what is lost if these individuals are transferred from the jurisdiction of the Board to the civil system? The PSRB certainly has more authority in managing mentally ill misdemeanants than the Mental Health and Developmental Disabilities Services Division (the Division) has in managing civilly committed patients. First, the period of jurisdiction under the Board is longer. A misdemeanant may be retained under the jurisdiction of the Board for up to 1 year compared with the 6-month limit on civil commitments in Oregon, although there are provisions in the civil commitment statutes for additional 6-month recommitments. The PSRB also has more power to achieve its goals in relation to the use of monitored conditional release. The Oregon civil commitment statutes (20) do make it possible to conditionally release a civilly committed patient from the hospital to a community mental health program, to monitor that individual in the community, and to revoke the conditional release. These powers are similar to those of the PSRB, and they were in fact drafted in recent years using the PSRB statutes as a model. These civil statutes have not been used as frequently as they might have been. We can speculate that the reason for this underutilization relates in part to legal questions about how much authority a community program actually has in relation to a conditionally released civil patient. However, at least on a conceptual level, it appears that the authority of the Board and the Division can be considered analogous. The major advantages that the PSRB has at this time are a longer period of jurisdiction over the individual and greater familiarity with the concept of conditional release and how to make it work effectively.

Are there disadvantages for the misdemeanants in the PSRB system? First, there is the question of stigma traditionally associated with mentally ill people (21, 22). The courts have recognized the power of stigma associated with civil commitment (23, 24) and with the criminal confinement of mentally ill patients (25). One could postulate a hierarchy of stigmatizing situations related to mental illness, starting from the voluntary outpatient on one end of the spectrum to the mentally ill offender in prison at the other end. However, insanity acquittees may fare the worst of all. They are a highly visible and controversial minority of mentally ill individuals, viewed as having "gotten off" their charges, beat the system with the help of disreputable forensic psychiatrists (26), and escaped punishment. In addition, they are generally portrayed as very dangerous. This perception is heightened by the celebrity nature of some insanity verdicts and unfortunate occurrences related to premature release, escape (27), or lack of community monitoring of some insanity acquittees.

Taking the issue of stigmatization into account would lend

further support to a significant goal of the mental health treatment system to treat individuals in the least restrictive manner possible. As an individual moves from the voluntary to the involuntary civil system to the criminal justice system, the stakes go up in the form of increased restrictions, the proliferation of negative stereotypes, and the lessening of individual autonomy. Thus, moving an individual further along this continuum should be undertaken with caution, and an unnecessary step should be avoided.

Returning to our focus on the Oregon system, these theoretical issues need to be viewed also from a practical viewpoint by highlighting how misdemeanants are managed once they are under the jurisdiction of the Board. Trial court judges placed significantly more misdemeanants than felons on conditional release at the time of assignment to PSRB jurisdiction. However, once in the hospital, the reverse occurred—the PSRB conditionally released significantly more felons than misdemeanants.

We have no clear explanation of the finding that the Board conditionally released so few misdemeanants once they were hospitalized. It is possible, given the limited duration of the Board's jurisdiction, that once hospitalized, the misdemeanant subjects were more likely to be overlooked in favor of individuals who were subject to longer periods of time under PSRB jurisdiction. We consider this to be an important question. We are interested in and intend to investigate how release decisions are made by the Board and how the forensic hospital staff works with the Board in developing conditional release plans for all hospitalized insanity acquittees, including misdemeanants.

We are reluctant to answer the question about whether misdemeanants should be continued under the jurisdiction of the PSRB. The PSRB system has a proven track record, although, as we have pointed out, there are some unanswered questions in relation to the management of misdemeanants under its jurisdiction. The civil commitment system has its own significant problems, wherein conflicts between rights, needs, and costs have yet to be resolved in a manner that provides effective modern treatment for individuals with serious mental illness. If civil commitment were less of a battlefield, it might be easier to answer the question of PSRB jurisdiction over misdemeanants.

REFERENCES

1. Foundation for Mental Health Services Research: Focus on Mental Health Services Research 5. Washington, DC, Foundation for Mental Health Services Research, November 1991

2. Teplin LA: The criminality of the mentally ill: a dangerous misconception. Am J Psychiatry 142:593–599, 1985

3. Teplin LA: The criminalization of the mentally ill: speculation in search of data. Psychol Bull 94:54–67, 1983

4. Zitrin A, Hardesty AS, Burdock EI, et al: Crime and violence among mental patients. Am J Psychiatry 133:142–149, 1976

5. Steadman HJ, Cocozza JJ, Melcik ME: Explaining the increased crime rate of mental patients: the changing clientele of state hospitals. Am J Psychiatry 135:33–42, 1978

6. Bloom JD, Faulkner LR, Shore JH, et al: The young adult chronic patient and the legal system: a system's analysis. New Dir Ment Health Serv 19:37–50, 1983

7. McFarland BH, Faulkner LR, Bloom JD, et al: Chronic mental illness and the criminal justice system. Hosp Community Psychiatry 40:718–723, 1989

8. Bloom JD, Shore JH, Arvidson B: Local variations in the arrests of psychiatric patients. Bull Am Acad Psychiatry Law 9:203–210, 1981

9. Miller RD: Involuntary Civil Commitment of the Mentally Ill in the Post-Reform Era. Springfield, IL, Charles C Thomas, 1987

10. Isaac RJ, Armat VC: Madness in the Streets—How Psychiatry and the Law Abandoned the Mentally Ill. New York, Free Press, 1990

11. Stone AA: Mental Health and Law: A System in Transition (DHEW Publ No ADM-76-176). Washington, DC, U.S. Government Printing Office, 1975

12. Lamb HR (ed): The Homeless Mentally Ill: A Task Force Report of the American Psychiatric Association. Washington, DC, American Psychiatric Association, 1984

13. Faulkner LR, Bloom JD, Resnick MR, et al: Local variations in the civil commitment process. Bull Am Acad Psychiatry Law 11:5–17, 1983

14. Faulkner LR, McFarland BH, Bloom JD: An empirical study of emergency commitment. Am J Psychiatry 146:182–187, 1989

15. Gudeman HE, Nelson MI, Kux LJ, et al: Changing admission patterns at Hawaii State Hospital following the 1976 revision of the Hawaii mental health statutes. Hawaii Med J 38:65–71, 1979

16. La Fond JQ, Durham ML: Back to Asylum: The Future of Mental Health Law and Policy in the United States. New York, Oxford University Press, 1992

17. ORS §161.327(1); modified by Oregon Laws, ch. 711, §2 (1981)

18. ORS §161.328; modified by Oregon Laws, ch. 711, §3 (1981)

19. Faulkner LR, McFarland BH, Bloom JD, et al: A methodology for predicting the effects of changes in civil commitment decision making. Bull Am Acad Psychiatry Law 14:71–80, 1986

20. Oregon Revised Statutes, Chapter 426, Mentally Ill and Sexually Dangerous

21. Fink PJ: Dealing with psychiatry's stigma. Hosp Community Psychiatry 37:814–818, 1986

22. Fink PJ, Tasman A (eds): Stigma and Mental Illness. Washington, DC, American Psychiatric Press, 1992

23. O'Connor v Donaldson, 442 US 563 (1975)

24. Addington v Texas, 441 US 418 (1978)

25. United States ex rel. Schuster v Herold, 410 F.2d 1071 (2d Cir. 1969)

26. Slater D, Hans VP: Public opinion of forensic psychiatry following the Hinckley verdict. Am J Psychiatry 141:675–679, 1984

27. Reichlin SM, Bloom JD: Effects of publicity on a forensic hospital. Paper presented at the annual meeting of the American Academy of Psychiatry and the Law, Boston, MA, October 1992

Chapter 10

Women and the Psychiatric Security Review Board

Relatively few papers in the literature discuss gender differences among insanity acquittees. Where data are available, women make up small percentages of insanity acquittee populations, with reported rates of 4% in Wyoming (1), 6% in Hawaii (2), 9% in Connecticut (3), 14% in New York (4, 5), and 18% in Illinois (6). In a review of the research literature on the insanity defense, Steadman estimated that approximately 10% of insanity acquittees are female (7).

Where comparisons have been made between women and men in these jurisdictions, women have been found to be acquitted of different kinds of crimes. For example, women show higher rates of acquittal for homicide crimes, and their victims are more likely to be family members (7). Additionally, reports generally agree that women have less involvement with the criminal justice system prior to the insanity judgment (8) and lower criminal recidivism rates (9).

Since the inception of the Psychiatric Security Review Board (PSRB) in 1978, 14% of the individuals placed under its jurisdiction have been women. In an earlier report from the first 4½ years of the PSRB (10), we compared 48 women with 384 men placed under the jurisdiction of the Board from 1978 to 1982. We found that women were clustered on both ends of the crime seriousness scale. On the one hand, a significantly greater percentage of women had insanity acquittals following charges of attempted homicides and homicide, whereas at the other end of the spectrum, women had been charged with a higher percentage of misdemeanor crimes. Women also were managed differently while under the Board's jurisdiction. When compared with men, the Board conditionally released women from the hospital after shorter stays and discharged women from its jurisdiction at a significantly higher rate.

In this chapter, we update and expand on earlier comparisons between women and men under the Board's jurisdiction, provide new information based on data collected for this study, and compare these findings with reports from other jurisdictions.

FEMALE AND MALE INSANITY ACQUITTEES AT THE TIME OF COMMITMENT TO THE PSRB

Demographics and Diagnosis

In the core research sample of 758 individuals, 106 (14%) were female and 652 (86%) were male. At the time of assignment to PSRB jurisdiction, women were significantly older than men, with an average age of 36 for women and 31 for men ($t = 3.75$, df = 740, $P = .0002$). There were no significant differences between women and men in terms of race, with both groups being predominantly white (91% of the women and 87% of the men).

We compared those subjects who did not complete high school with those who had completed high school and those with some post-high school education. Although approximately half of both groups did not complete high school, women had more education than men, with 41% of the women having some education beyond high school compared with 21% of the men ($\chi^2 = 7.30$, df = 2, $P = .0260$). Approximately 10% of both groups were married, but women were much less likely to be single (31% of the women compared with 64% of the men) and more likely to be widowed, separated, or divorced (58% of the women compared with 26% of the men; $\chi^2 = 36.76$, df = 2, $P = .0000$).

Table 10–1 presents diagnostic information based on gender. There were no significant differences between the major diagnostic categories. However, within some categories we did find differences. Although 75% of the females and 71% of the males had a diagnosis of psychosis, women were more likely to be diagnosed with bipolar disorder and men were more likely to be diagnosed with schizophrenia ($\chi^2 = 23.53$, df = 2, $P = .0000$). Similarly, women and men had comparable rates of diagnosis of personality disorder. However, when we compared antisocial, borderline, and other personality disorders combined, we found that women were more likely to be diagnosed as borderline and men were more likely to be diagnosed as antisocial (χ^2 = 19.54, df = 2, P = .0001).

Crime Leading to Placement Under PSRB Jurisdiction

As presented in Table 10–2, there were differences between the two groups in the crime leading to PSRB jurisdiction. Although most of both groups were assigned to the PSRB for felony crimes, trial courts assigned a significantly greater percentage of women as the result of a misdemeanor charge. Sixty-five percent of the women had been charged with a felony compared with 74% of the men (χ^2 = 4.0, df = 1, P = .0454).

Within the felony and misdemeanor categories, there were also differences in the types of crimes leading to PSRB jurisdiction. As seen in Table 10–2, the most frequent felony charges for women were assault, arson, and manslaughter. For men, the

Table 10–1.   Gender differences in diagnosis

Diagnosis	Females (n = 91)	%	Males (n = 606)	%
Psychosis	68	75	431	71
Schizophrenia	48	53	373	62
Bipolar disorder	17	19	29	5
Other psychosis	3	3	29	5
Mental retardation	6	7	50	8
Organic brain disorder	2	2	30	5
Personality disorder	9	10	66	11
Borderline	6	7	6	1
Antisocial	1	1	22	4
Schizoid	1	1	8	1
Paranoid			8	1
Inadequate			7	1
Other	1	1	15	2
Other diagnosis	2	2	12	2
Substance abuse	4	4	17	3

most frequent felony charges leading to PSRB jurisdiction were assault, burglary, and unauthorized use of a motor vehicle. Within the misdemeanor category, there were fewer differences between women and men. Trial court judges assigned both female and male misdemeanants most often for menacing or harassment.

Although a large percentage of the female population raised a successful insanity defense on charges of homicide or attempted

Table 10–2. Category of crime leading to PSRB jurisdiction

Crime category	Females (n = 106)		Males (n = 652)	
	Frequency	%	Frequency	%
Felony crimes	69	65	485	74
Assault	16	15	82	13
Arson	12	11	44	7
Manslaughter	8	8	4	1
Attempted homicide	6	6	13	2
Robbery	4	4	42	6
Kidnapping	4	4	8	1
Sexual assault	3	3	53	8
Burglary	3	3	78	12
Unauthorized use of motor vehicle (UUV)	2	2	68	10
Murder	2	2	20	3
Theft	2	2	15	2
Other felony	7	7	58	9
Misdemeanor crimes	37	35	167	26
Menacing/harassment	9	8	71	11
Criminal mischief	7	7	13	2
Driving offenses	5	5	8	1
Theft/attempted UUV	4	4	21	3
Trespass/attempted burglary	3	3	16	2
Arson/reckless burning	3	3	5	1
Resisting arrest	2	2	12	2
Sexual offenses	1	1	15	2
Weapons offenses	1	1	6	1
Other misdemeanor	2	2		

homicide, women and men also differed in the types of homicide charges. Table 10–3 shows the breakdown of homicide and attempted homicide charges for women and men. Women were most likely to have been charged with manslaughter, whereas men were most likely to have been charged with murder.

When we compared the average seriousness score of only those subjects with felony crimes leading to PSRB jurisdiction, women had an average seriousness score of 323, which was significantly more serious than the average score of 348 for men (t = 2.071, df = 550, P =.0389). Thus, although women were less likely to be assigned to the PSRB for felony crimes, they committed, on average, more serious felony crimes compared with men.

Prior Experience With the Criminal Justice System

There were a number of differences between the two groups in their prior experience with the criminal justice system. Overall, women were significantly less likely to have had prior contacts with the criminal justice system; 54% of the females and 81% of the males had some prior criminal justice contact (χ^2 = 37.16, df = 1, P = .0000). Female subjects had an average of 2.3 prior criminal justice contacts—significantly less than the male subjects, who had an average of 4.4 prior contacts (t = 6.64, df = 756, P = .0000). When these prior contacts were adjusted for time and age at assignment to the PSRB, there was still a significant difference between the two groups. Females had an average of 0.24 contacts per adult year and males had an average of 0.53 contacts per adult year (t = 4.007, df = 752, P = .0001).

Table 10–3.   Homicide crimes leading to PSRB jurisdiction

	Female (n = 10)	%	Male (n = 24)	%
Manslaughter I	7	70	4	17
Murder	1	10	18	75
Felony murder	1	10		
Manslaughter II	1	10		
Conspiracy murder			2	8

Table 10–4 shows the nature of these prior criminal contacts. We compared the overall rate of felony and misdemeanor contacts and found that women were involved in significantly fewer prior felony contacts than men—33% compared with 48% (χ^2 = 13.71, df = 1, P = .0002). We again noted differences in

Table 10–4. Criminal justice contacts prior to PSRB

Crime category	Females (n = 163)		Males (n = 2,320)	
	Frequency	%	Frequency	%
Felony crimes	54	33	1,116	48
Escape/failure to appear	11	7	86	4
Assault	10	6	182	8
Arson	10	6	33	1
Drug offenses	7	4	134	6
Burglary	3	2	206	9
Unauthorized use of motor vehicle	3	2	74	3
Theft	2	1	122	5
Criminal mischief	2	1	68	3
Murder	1	1	4	< 1
Attempted murder	1	1	4	< 1
Sexual assault	1	1	36	2
Robbery			85	4
Driving offenses			23	1
Kidnapping			10	< 1
Weapons offenses			3	< 1
Other felony	3	2	46	2
Misdemeanor crimes	109	67	1,204	52
Theft	40	25	344	15
Trespass	27	17	144	6
Resisting arrest	11	7	117	5
Menacing/harassment	7	4	177	8
Driving offenses	6	4	194	8
Criminal mischief	6	4	53	2
Sexual offenses	4	2	48	2
Escape/failure to appear	2	1	50	2
Weapons offenses	2	1	43	2
Arson	1	1	7	< 1
Other misdemeanor	3	2	27	1

the rates of contacts for particular crime categories, especially in the burglary, robbery, and theft contacts. Altogether, 28% of the contacts for women and 33% of the contacts for men were in these categories. However, women were most often charged with misdemeanor theft and men with felony burglary, theft, and robbery. When we compared the average seriousness score of the prior felony charges, there was no significant difference between women and men.

Prior Experience With the Mental Health System

We compared the two groups in terms of prior state mental hospitalizations. There was no significant difference in the number of subjects with a prior hospitalization: 74% of the women and 77% of the men had at least one hospitalization prior to assignment to the PSRB. Women had more hospital episodes, with an average of 4.2 hospital episodes compared with 2.9 for men ($t = 2.99$, df = 756, $P = .0029$).

Because of the limitations with community service data, we selected a subsample of individuals assigned to the PSRB between 1983 and 1986 and looked at community service utilization in the 2 years prior to assignment. There were few differences between the two groups in this area. Most subjects had some involvement with the community mental health system in this time period (82% of the women and 76% of the men). This experience was primarily in the form of outpatient treatment services (56% of the women and 54% of the men) and precommitment services (49% of the women and 33% of the men). For this subsample, 73% of the women and 70% of the men were hospitalized during the 2 years prior to the PSRB. When we combined hospital and community service utilization data, we found that 98% of the women and 90% of the men had some contact with the state mental health system in the 2 years prior to the PSRB.

Prior Experience With Mental Health and Criminal Justice Systems

For the total sample, we combined the prior experience with the criminal justice and hospital mental health systems and found a significant difference in overall experience as seen in Figure 10–1 (χ^2 = 39.217, df = 3, P = .0000). Most of the women and men had prior contact in both the criminal justice and mental health systems, although the percentage of women having such contacts was much lower than for the men. The main difference is that women were less likely than men to have prior contact in the criminal justice system, either with or without contact in the mental health system.

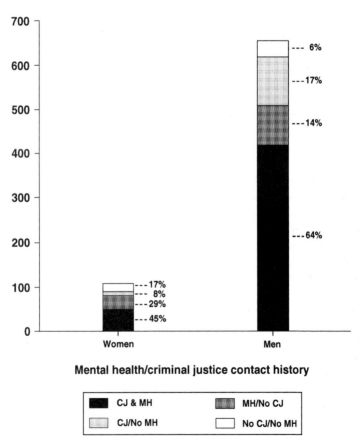

Figure 10–1. Prior mental health (MH) and/or criminal justice (CJ) contacts by gender.

FEMALE AND MALE INSANITY ACQUITTEES UNDER PSRB JURISDICTION

As we discussed in Chapter 4, trial court judges were significantly more likely to place women in the community instead of in the hospital as the initial placement under the PSRB. Judges assigned 36% of the females and 19% of the males to an initial community placement ($\chi^2 = 15.72$, df = 1, $P = .0001$). For those subjects the judges initially placed in the hospital, the Board was significantly more likely to place women than men on conditional release. Of the 597 initially hospitalized subjects, the Board conditionally released 49% of the females and 35% of the males ($\chi^2 = 4.50$, df = 1, $P = .0339$).

Overall, combining conditional release by courts and the Board, 67% of the female subjects and 48% of the male subjects spent part of the study time in the community ($\chi^2 = 13.78$, df = 1, $P = .0002$). Of those subjects with some conditional release time, there was no significant difference between females and males in the rate of revocation of conditional release, with 42% of the females and 49% of the males being revoked during the study period. However, women remained on conditional release significantly longer prior to this first revocation. For women, revocation occurred following an average of 16 months on conditional release, compared with an average of 10 months on conditional release for men ($t = 2.16$, df = 180, $P = .0323$).

When we compared the total amount of PSRB time spent in the hospital and on conditional release, these gender differences continue to be reflected. Female subjects spent an average of 16 months on conditional release and 11 months in the hospital, with 52% of their time under the PSRB, or of the study period, in the hospital. Each of these figures is significantly different for males, who spent an average of 11 months on conditional release ($t = 2.83$, df = 756, $P = .0047$), 19 months in the hospital ($t = 3.81$, df = 756, $P = .0002$), and 71% of their PSRB time in the hospital ($t = 4.84$, df = 756, $P = .0000$).

Because of the higher proportion of misdemeanants in the female group, we wanted to explore whether the different amounts of time in the hospital and on conditional release were associated primarily with gender, with the type of crime leading to PSRB jurisdiction, or with some combination of the two factors. As shown in Table 10–5, we divided the sample into four groups: female felons, female misdemeanants, male felons, and male misdemeanants. For total time under PSRB jurisdiction, the only differences were for the felony-misdemeanor comparisons, and there were no gender differences within the two crime-type groups.

When we conducted post-hoc comparisons for amount of time in the hospital and on conditional release in the community, we found that in addition to the differences between felons and misdemeanants, there were gender differences within the felony group. Female felons spent significantly less time in the hospital than male felons (post-hoc t test, $P = .0001$) and significantly more time on conditional release (post-hoc t test, $P = .0000$). The comparison for the percentage of PSRB time spent in the hospital suggests that the group of female felons accounts for most of the differences we found in this area. There were no differences in the comparisons between female felons and female misdemeanants, between male felons and male misdemeanants, or between female misdemeanants and male misdemeanants. However, female felons spent a significantly smaller percentage of their PSRB time in the hospital than male felons (post-hoc t test, $P = .0000$) or male misdemeanants (post-hoc t test, $P = .0000$).

Table 10–5.   Time in months under PSRB jurisdiction and placement

	Female		Male	
	Felon ($n = 69$)	Misdemeanant ($n = 37$)	Felon ($n = 485$)	Misdemeanant ($n = 167$)
Time under PSRB[a]	36	11	37	11
Time in hospital[b]	14	6	23	7
Time in community[c]	22	5	12	5
% PSRB time in hospital[d]	48	59	71	72

[a] $F = 57.57$, df = 3,754, $P = .0000$.
[b] $F = 36.44$, df = 3,754, $P = .0000$.
[c] $F = 21.08$, df = 3,754, $P = .0000$.
[d] $F = 8.40$, df = 3,754, $P = .0000$.

As we have discussed in earlier chapters, there were few contacts with the criminal justice system during PSRB jurisdiction. Table 10–6 presents the nature of these contacts for women and men. As we discussed in Chapter 4, most police contacts during

Table 10–6.   Criminal justice contacts during the PSRB

Crime category	Females (n = 5)		Males (n = 100)	
	Frequency	%	Frequency	%
Felony crimes	1	20	55	55
Sex abuse	1	20	1	1
Burglary/robbery/theft			22	22
Assault			6	6
Drugs			5	5
Unauthorized use of motor vehicle			4	4
Eluding a police officer			4	4
Failure to appear			3	3
Rape			2	2
Felony driving while suspended			2	2
Homicide			2	2
Criminal mischief			1	1
Intimidation			1	1
Perjury			1	1
Arson			1	1
Misdemeanor crimes	4	80	45	45
Driving under the influence	2	40	9	9
Theft	1	20	17	17
Criminal mischief	1	20	1	1
Assault			7	7
Driving offenses			3	3
Menacing/harassment			3	3
Trespass			1	1
Public Indecency			1	1
Reckless endangerment			1	1
Failure to pay fine			1	1
Resisting arrest			1	1
Escape	10		57	

PSRB jurisdiction were associated with escapes, many of which may reflect revocations from conditional release and not new criminal contacts. Overall, the escapes made up 67% of the total contacts for women and 36% of the total contacts for men. When we examined the remaining contacts, women had a single felony contact for sex abuse and four misdemeanor contacts for driving under the influence, criminal mischief, and theft. Men had 55 felony contacts, primarily for burglary/robbery/theft, and 45 misdemeanor contacts, primarily for theft and driving under the influence.

Finally, we examined discharges from PSRB jurisdiction. By the end of the study period, 52% of the female subjects and 56% of the male subjects had been discharged. There were no differences in the two groups in terms of the rate of discharge or the reasons for discharge. One women died, compared with 7 men who died of natural causes and 13 who committed suicide. The appellate courts ordered the discharge of seven men for other reasons, such as failure of the Board to hold a mandatory hearing or the reversal of the original conviction and assignment to the PSRB. The Board discharged 42% of the women and 40% of the men because the period of PSRB jurisdiction had elapsed. The Board also ordered discretionary discharges for 56% of the females and 52% of the males based on a Board finding that the subjects were no longer mentally ill or no longer dangerous. Among the discretionary discharges, the Board found more women to be no longer dangerous (90% of discretionary discharges) when compared with men (76% of discretionary discharges). This difference was not significant.

FEMALE AND MALE INSANITY ACQUITTEES FOLLOWING DISCHARGE FROM THE PSRB

We selected a sample of 261 subjects discharged between 1981 and 1985 so as to have adequate data on utilization of community mental health services and at least 1 year of follow-up during the study period. Of these 261 subjects, 34 (13%) were female and 227 (87%) were male, percentages similar to the overall PSRB population.

Mental Health Service Utilization Following the PSRB

We examined the use of state mental health services following discharge from PSRB jurisdiction and found few significant differences in the use of hospital and community services between women and men in this sample.

There were no significant differences in overall rates of hospitalization, but there were differences in the total number of days that women and men spent in the hospital. During the follow-up period, 56% of the women and 66% of the men spent some time in the hospital. Women spent an average of 19 days hospitalized compared with 74 days for the men. Neither of these comparisons was significantly different. However, when we controlled for the variable amounts of follow-up time, females spent only 3% of the follow-up time in the hospital compared with 15% for males ($t = 2.567$, df = 259, $P = .0108$).

Most subjects received some community mental health service in the follow-up period. Seventy-six percent of the females and 66% of the males had some community mental health system involvement. Women, on average, spent 30% of their follow-up time enrolled in some community service, compared with 28% for men. There were no significant differences in the types of community services received when we examined outpatient, residential, and precommitment services.

Criminal Justice Experience Following the PSRB

As with criminal justice contacts before the PSRB, we found that female subjects had fewer contacts with the criminal justice system after discharge than did male subjects. Only 26% of the female subjects had any involvement with the criminal justice system during the follow-up period, compared with 51% of the male subjects ($\chi^2 = 7.19$, df = 1, $P = .0073$). Females had an average of 0.1 criminal justice contacts per follow-up year compared with 0.4 for males ($t = 2.22$, df = 258, $P = .0274$).

There was no significant difference between women and men when we compared the rate of felony versus misdemeanor contacts. For women, 29% of the post-PSRB contacts involved felony crimes, compared with 44% for the men. However, there again were differences between women and men in their involvement in certain types of crimes. The combined categories of robbery, theft, and burglary accounted for 10% of the females' post-PSRB contacts and 37% of the males' contacts. Trespass and misdemeanor criminal mischief accounted for 24% of the females' post-PSRB contacts and 9% of the males' contacts.

DISCUSSION

The results of the comparisons for this larger sample of women and men were very much in line with our earlier study of women under PSRB jurisdiction in 1978–1982 (10). Although we found a number of changes, there were no surprising variations from the earlier study. There was a slight increase in the proportion of female PSRB clients—from 11% in the earlier study to 14% for the present sample. Also, in the earlier study we found that the trial court judges assigned 42% of the women to the jurisdiction of the PSRB as a result of misdemeanor charges. For this larger sample, the proportion of women with misdemeanor charges was reduced to 35%. These findings suggest that in recent years, the trial court judges assigned more women to the PSRB for more serious crimes than earlier in the Board's existence.

As we found in the earlier study, significantly more women had time on conditional release and spent less time hospitalized. Both trial court judges and the Board were more likely to conditionally release women than men. Once conditionally released, there was no difference in the rate of revocation although women remained on conditional release longer prior to revocation. Overall, women spent much less of their PSRB time in the hospital compared with men (52% and 71%, respectively). As depicted in Table 10–5, the primary difference between women and men appears to be in the manner in which the PSRB manages female felons: they spend less of their PSRB time in the hospital and more time on conditional release than either male felons or misdemeanants.

Unlike the earlier study, we found no difference in the rate of discretionary discharges from PSRB jurisdiction. This may be a result of the overall decrease in the rate of discretionary discharges from 1983 through the end of the study period, as discussed in Chapter 5.

We were able to examine a number of new areas in this chapter with data now available on the utilization of state mental health services and subjects' involvement with the criminal justice system. There were few differences between women and men regarding involvement with the mental health system prior to assignment to PSRB jurisdiction. Although women had more hospital episodes than men, they did not actually spend more time in the hospital. For those subjects in our discharge subsample, there were no differences in the use of community mental health services, but women spent significantly less of the follow-up time in the hospital than men.

Women in our sample were significantly older than men, better educated, and more likely to be married. Overall, there were no diagnostic differences in the major diagnostic categories, although there was a significant difference within the psychosis category. For both women and men, schizophrenia was the predominant diagnosis. However, there were significantly more diagnoses of bipolar disorder among women than among men. Some of the demographic differences may be partially explained by diagnosis. When compared to patients with schizophrenia, patients with bipolar disorder are more likely to be married and better educated.

The differences within the personality disorder diagnoses reflect gender differences seen in this area, with women having significantly more diagnoses of borderline personality disorder and men more diagnoses of antisocial personality disorder. It also is interesting to note an apparent absence of "soft diagnoses" for women such as "battered women's syndrome" or "depressive neurosis," despite the fact that the use of these diagnoses has received a great deal of attention in the media and the literature. This may be due in part to the fact that we collected diagnostic data from state hospital and community mental health programs and that these data may not reflect what diagnostic formulation was presented at trial. Issues related to diagnosis are discussed in more detail in Chapter 8.

Differences in involvement with the criminal justice system, both before and after PSRB jurisdiction, were in keeping with much of the data reported in the criminal justice literature and reports on insanity acquittees in other jurisdictions. Women had less prior involvement with the criminal justice system, and when they were involved, the crimes were generally different. Women were much less likely to be charged with felony crimes of theft, robbery, and/or burglary.

When we examined the crime leading to assignment to PSRB jurisdiction, we found important differences between women and men. We found that the women's crimes tend to cluster at both ends of the seriousness scale. A larger percentage of the women were assigned for homicide-related offenses and for misdemeanors. There was a striking difference between women and men in the homicide category. Women raised the insanity defense most often for the lesser charges of manslaughter, whereas men were most often charged with murder. We do not know if the factual situations leading to these different charges were actually different for the female and male subjects or if the results reflect differences in the way the criminal justice system handles women and men. This question would await further study.

Although the study sample was predominantly male, the percentage of women under the jurisdiction of the PSRB was generally higher when compared with the reports from other jurisdictions presented earlier. One reason for this higher percentage of women in our data as compared with other jurisdictions may be the inclusion in the PSRB of individuals charged with misdemeanor offenses. Other jurisdictions provide alternative dispositions for individuals raising an insanity defense in response to misdemeanor charges (11), and such individuals may not be represented in the reports from other jurisdictions.

The number of female insanity acquittees is also higher when compared with other criminal justice populations. On June 30, 1984, only 7% of the jail population in the United States was female (12). Similarly, only 4% of the prisoners in state and federal institutions were female as of the last day of 1983, 1984, and 1985 (13).

In summary, we found differences in our comparisons of women and men before, during, and after their time under PSRB jurisdiction. It is hard to know at this point whether these findings reflect basic differences between the sexes, reflect differences in how women and men are handled by the system all along the way, or both. The ability to make such distinctions would require more of an emphasis on the "careers" of women and men, most of whom have serious mental illness and multiple involvements with the mental health and criminal justice systems.

REFERENCES

1. Pasewark R, Lanthorn B: Disposition of persons utilizing the insanity plea in a rural state. East Tennessee State University Journal of Humanics 5:87–99, 1977
2. Bogenberger RP, Pasewark RA, Gudeman H, et al: Follow-up of insanity acquittees in Hawaii. Int J Law Psychiatry 10:283–295, 1987
3. Zonana HV, Bartel RL, Wells JA, et al: Sex differences in person found not guilty by reason of insanity: analysis of data from the Connecticut NGRI registry. Bull Am Acad Psychiatry Law 18:129–142, 1990
4. Steadman HJ: Insanity acquittals in New York State: 1965–1978. Am J Psychiatry 137:321–326, 1980
5. Pasewark RA, Pantle ML, Steadman HJ: Characteristics and disposition of persons found not guilty by reason of insanity in New York State, 1971–1976. Am J Psychiatry 136:655–660, 1979
6. Wettstein RM, Mulvey EP: Disposition of insanity acquittees in Illinois. Bull Am Acad Psychiatry Law 16:11–24, 1988
7. Steadman HJ: Empirical research on the insanity defense. Annual of the American Academy of Political and Social Science 477:58–71, 1985
8. Pasewark RA: Insanity plea: a review of the research literature. Journal of Psychiatry and the Law 9:357–402, 1982
9. Pantle ML, Pasewark RA, Steadman HJ: Comparing institutionalization periods and subsequent arrests of insanity acquittees and convicted felons. Journal of Psychiatry and the Law 8:305–316, 1980
10. Rogers JL, Sack WH, Bloom JD, et al: Women in Oregon's insanity defense system. Journal of Psychiatry and the Law, Winter 1983, pp 515–532
11. Weiner B: Mental disability and criminal law, in The Mentally Disabled and the Law, 3rd Edition. Edited by Brakel S, Parry J, Weiner B. Chicago, IL, American Bar Foundation, 1985, pp 707–729

12. U.S. Department of Justice, Bureau of Justice, Statistics: Jail Inmates 1984 (Bulletin NCJ-101094). Washington, DC, U.S. Department of Justice, May 1986, p 2, Table 3
13. U.S. Department of Justice, Bureau of Justice, Statistics: Prisoners in 1983, Bulletin NCJ-92949, p 2; Prisoners in 1984 (Bulletin NCJ-97118), p 2; Prisoners in 1985 (Bulletin NCJ-101384), p 2. Washington, DC, U.S. Department of Justice, 1983–1985

Chapter 11

Financial Aspects of the Psychiatric Security Review Board

Bentson H. McFarland, M.D., Ph.D.
Douglas A. Bigelow, Ph.D.

There are important reasons for examining financial aspects of the Psychiatric Security Review Board (PSRB). Planners considering adoption of such a system need information about budgetary impacts. Policymakers may wish to compare costs and effects of a program such as the PSRB with those of other programs for mentally ill offenders. In this chapter, we address three financial aspects of the PSRB: administrative costs of the Board itself, costs and effects of programs for monitored conditional release to the community, and the impact of an entitlement program within a relatively fixed total mental health care budget.

As demonstrated in this book, the PSRB has been shown to be effective in dealing with a difficult group of forensic patients. The greatest level of interest in the program has come from families of mentally ill individuals who have been involved with the criminal justice system and from forensic mental health professionals. In addition to interest in program design, both groups have been very interested in the fiscal requirements of a PSRB-type program—especially when working with legislative and administrative bodies who must be convinced that this investment will be worthwhile. We describe those fiscal requirements below.

In our experience, mental health administrators have viewed the program ambivalently, especially in relation to inpatient services. Some policymakers associate the PSRB with what was, until 1986, an escalating forensic inpatient census (see Chapter 5). Conversely, mental health administrators have shown considerable interest in the conditional release mechanisms developed by the Board. Conditional release provides a means of reducing the number and length of inpatient stays—an important concern for any mental health program in an era of severe fiscal constraints (1). Administrators considering the implementation of analogous systems for managing insanity acquittees are therefore very interested in the costs and effectiveness of PSRB's monitoring and supervisory functions that permit conditional release to outpatient programs. In this chapter, we examine in some detail the financial implications of community versus hospital placement for acquittees.

Mental health administrators also have expressed concerns about the impact on their system when the PSRB is viewed as a type of entitlement program that might displace services from other groups of mentally ill individuals. This is also discussed.

ADMINISTRATIVE COSTS ASSOCIATED WITH OREGON'S PSRB

As we described in Chapter 1, the system developed in Oregon has two major components: one associated with operation of the Board itself and the other associated with treatment provided to insanity acquittees by the Mental Health and Developmental Disabilities Services Division (the Division). From a fiscal viewpoint, costs are distributed between these state agencies, and each is discussed here. There has been relatively little published about the economic impact of this system. Indeed, detailed reporting and discussion of the actual costs of delivering specific mental health services to defined target populations are not commonly found in the literature (2).

Bigelow and colleagues (3) examined the PSRB budget in detail. We refer extensively to this paper, as we believe it is the only study pertaining to the financial aspects of such a system (4).

Although the Oregon Legislature vested a great deal of power in the Board, the study by Bigelow and colleagues demonstrated that the associated administrative overhead was quite small. The

PSRB functions with administrative and clerical staff of approximately three full-time equivalent (FTE) employees. The Board (as described in Chapter 1) comprises five part-time appointees who are paid on a level comparable with other members of voluntary statewide boards and commissions. Therefore, the administrative costs are very low, but it is the expenditures associated with clinical services (i.e., the hospital and community treatment programs, which are discussed in the next section) that represent the greatest costs associated with the PSRB system.

COSTS AND EFFECTS OF MONITORED CONDITIONAL RELEASE

The Division is responsible for the costs for treatment of insanity acquittees in the forensic hospital and in the community. Thus, there are costs associated with both inpatient and community components. In fact, the program is predominantly inpatient-oriented, because acquittees spend, on average, approximately 68% of their PSRB time in the hospital (see Chapter 4). However, the community component of PSRB is extremely important because (among the other reasons explored in this book) there may be substantial cost savings associated with use of monitored outpatient programs for insanity acquittees.

Bigelow and colleagues (3) pointed out that in 1987, the Division's expenditures for inpatient treatment were approximately $98 per day compared with outpatient costs of $13 per day. These expenditure data illuminate the fiscal impact of the PSRB's outpatient component. It was estimated that if outpatient programs for insanity acquittees were eliminated, the state would then have to increase its 1987 forensic mental health expenditures by 28% to accommodate an additional 99 forensic inpatients (see the Endnote for discussion of cost computation methodology).

By definition, the financial impact calculations performed in this study are applicable within the PSRB system. It is also reasonable to consider the impact of the PSRB on the larger public mental health environment.

IMPACT OF THE PSRB AS AN ENTITLEMENT PROGRAM

It is important to distinguish between benefits the Division provides for specified individuals under the jurisdiction of the PSRB and the operation of most of the other public mental health programs in Oregon. The provision of mental health services to insanity acquittees under the jurisdiction of the Board can be considered a categorical system in which clients are identified by a particular legal status and subsequently are entitled to specific benefits both in the hospital and in the community.

While under the jurisdiction of the PSRB, acquittees are entitled to a variety of inpatient and/or outpatient services (i.e., those ordered by the Board). These services are financed from the overall mental health budget. From an accounting perspective, services to acquittees are viewed as a separate entity in the Division's appropriation from the state legislature. However, because the total mental health budget is relatively fixed, expenditures for acquittees may effectively subtract resources from other Division programs. Two examples illustrate this point. When the PSRB was created, the legislature specifically funded the conditional release component of the program with a separate budget. This is an example of "new" money coming into the system. On the other hand, on several occasions, when the inpatient population was increasing, the Legislative Assembly mandated that the Division internally reallocate funds to cover the increased inpatient census for these mandated acquittees.

The latter situation thus had ramifications for the rest of the public mental health system. On the one hand, since 1985, the state mental hospital in Oregon serving the catchment area with the largest population base was closed to voluntary inpatients in favor of those who have been civilly committed (another entitlement program). In contrast, insanity acquittees under the jurisdiction of the PSRB automatically were admitted or readmitted when the Board made a judgment that hospitalization was indicated. The hospital system in Oregon was thus skewed in the direction of involuntary care for civilly committed patients and for insanity acquittees. Those mentally ill individuals willing to accept voluntary inpatient treatment were unable to obtain this care in the state mental health system. In the arena of hospital services, involuntary patients' entitlement has led to displacement of other potential clients who were willing to accept treatment voluntarily.

As discussed in Chapter 9 in relation to misdemeanants, this problem may be self-perpetuating, because there was an incentive for the advocates of mentally ill individuals to seek the service entitlement conferred by involuntary status. There are anecdotal reports and some survey data about individuals being advised to press criminal charges against mentally ill persons in order to obtain the PSRB entitlement (5), because this was viewed as a more effective route to treatment than civil commitment.

As described in Chapter 6, services provided to insanity acquittees on conditional release in the community are comparable with treatment offered other groups of mentally ill individuals. Most of Oregon's public mental health programs effectively operate under a "programmatic" system in which services are provided to individuals meeting eligibility criteria on a first-come, first-served basis. For example, community support programs are available chiefly to individuals with chronic disabling mental disorders such as schizophrenia who, without treatment, are at risk for hospitalization. The Division estimates that it serves roughly half of the persons in Oregon who meet eligibility criteria for community support (6). There is a waiting list for community support services and for other community mental health programs, particularly in Oregon's metropolitan areas.

PSRB community services operate in a similar manner. The Division funds a number of "slots" for conditionally released insanity acquittees under the jurisdiction of the Board. As we described in Chapter 1, conditional release will not be granted if a suitable community placement is unavailable. The individual may have to wait in the hospital until a slot opens.

However, the waiting list for conditional release programs is usually short, because the Division has a great deal of flexibility with its PSRB community slots. In contrast to other aspects of the community support program, PSRB slots are not fixed within a county system, and the Division can transfer them between counties. Also, in some circumstances, the Division can use funds earmarked for other community support programs to create

PSRB community slots. On the other hand, the absence of providers willing to supervise insanity acquittees may limit the numbers of PSRB slots that can be established.

There are significant financial differences between PSRB slots and "regular" (nonforensic) community support programs. In the 1990–1991 fiscal year, providers were paid about $3,600 for each community support slot, whereas the rate for a PSRB "basic" slot was some $3,900 (7). The extra funding for the PSRB is intended to compensate the provider for the required monthly report to the PSRB as well as other administrative activities necessitated by problems acquittees may encounter in the community.

More important than the PSRB "basic" slot rate is the extra funding available for hard-to-place PSRB clients. In essence, the Division can increase the PSRB basic slot rate by purchasing residential services. A few PSRB clients who are very hard to place occupied slots that cost the Division approximately $25,000 annually in 1990. The 1989 session of the Legislative Assembly appropriated funds for 30 hard-to-place insanity acquittees at the rate of $19,000 annually (8). Conversely, the Division paid providers of community support services to "regular" (nonforensic) clients about $3,600 annually for outpatient programs and roughly $7,400 for residential services in 1990 (7). State-funded capacity in 1990 for regular community support programs was 4,486 community support slots and 1,889 residential slots. On average, then, regular community support clients cost the Division about $6,700 annually in 1990. These figures are approximate, because two or more regular community support clients can "occupy" one outpatient treatment slot. Conversely, in some instances the Division may allow a residential provider to bill for empty beds in order to cover unexpected costs. In any event, these calculations show that, on a per-individual-served basis, acquittees on conditional release are funded at a higher rate than are clients of regular community support programs.

DISCUSSION

Given that the budget for the public mental health system is controlled by the legislature and is less than adequate to serve all who might conceivably benefit from its services, there is a substantial impact of the PSRB on the rest of the system. From one perspective, the PSRB can be viewed as drawing funds from nonentitled clients and redirecting those dollars to entitled insanity acquittees. It is worth exploring the implications of this type of categorical funding.

First, it should be noted that the typical PSRB client shares many characteristics with individuals involved in civil commitment and in other programs of the public mental health system. Of course, by definition, PSRB clients have committed a felony or misdemeanor. However, as has been documented here, many chronically mentally ill individuals have involvement with the criminal justice system (9). Indeed, in some cases, it is simply a matter of chance whether an individual with severe mental illness who commits a crime will end up in the criminal justice or the mental health system. However, persons with severe mental illness who are monitored by the PSRB are entitled to more services than might be available for similar persons enrolled in the public mental health system.

Advocacy groups (particularly family members of persons with severe mental illness) have suggested that it may be preferable for chronically mentally ill individuals to become involved with the criminal justice system because "at last they will get some help" (9). In some sense, then, PSRB entitlements might be considered as emphasizing that a significant route to mental health care is through "criminal behavior."

Another consequence of the PSRB system is the inevitable flow of funds toward treatment and away from prevention. Although it is true that primary prevention of severe mental illness such as schizophrenia is not currently feasible, there is growing evidence that secondary prevention may be worthwhile. Several studies (10) indicate the value of early treatment for schizophrenia in terms of reducing the tendency to develop chronic psychosis. However, in a public mental health system focused on the decompensated chronically mentally ill person, it may not be possible for persons with prodromal symptoms of schizophrenia or early psychosis to obtain treatment. Rather, funds are directed preferentially toward serving those who are most severely ill. The entitlement aspect of the PSRB and, more important, of civil commitment are examples of this phenomenon.

The PSRB system is an attempt to balance the offender's need for treatment against society's need for protection. Policymakers reviewing systems such as the PSRB need to include in their deliberations questions relating to financial aspects of the program. The costs of outpatient as opposed to inpatient services need to be balanced against society's need for protection from dangerous patients. One also must consider the appropriate distribution of limited resources in terms of treating severely ill individuals versus preventing further deterioration among those who are less impaired. Finally, it is important to recognize that an entitlement program such as the PSRB will inevitably have an impact on other parts of the government's public mental health system.

It may be possible to take a (semi)quantitative approach to balancing the needs for treatment and protection with cost considerations. Much work in the area of medical cost-effectiveness is based on computing the dollar costs necessary per "year of life saved" (11). Examples of these calculations include a cost per year of life saved of $4,500 (in 1983) for neonatal intensive care with infants weighing more than 1 kilogram and $54,000 (in 1983) per year of life saved for hospital hemodialysis (12).

For the PSRB, the analogous computation might be cost per felony or misdemeanor prevented. To perform these calculations, one would need to know the acquittees' baseline rate of offending (e.g., felonies per year) and the rates of offending for PSRB clients in the inpatient and outpatient components of the program. One would next subtract the "PSRB offending rate" from the "baseline offending rate" to determine the "rate of prevented offenses." Actual costs of the inpatient and outpatient components of the program could then be used to compute the "cost per offense prevented" for both the inpatient and outpatient components of the PSRB. Clearly, in such a study one would need to understand the economic costs of inpatient and outpatient programs for this population (13).

Economic analyses of programs such as the PSRB are just beginning. We anticipate much work in this area as the cost-benefit ratios of long-term versus episodic care come more to the fore. The data available in relation to the PSRB will be used to begin to develop our understanding of the interface between mental health programming and economics.

CONCLUSION

It should be noted that the fiscal impact approach used by Bigelow and colleagues (3) is based on the concept of average cost per client in either inpatient or outpatient programs. This methodology is indeed appropriate when considering wholesale establishment or abolition of treatment systems (such as the outpatient component of the PSRB). An alternative approach attempts to estimate the marginal impact of moving just one client from one program to another. The marginal methodology may be more appropriate when attempting to estimate the financial impact of shifting a small number of clients (e.g., from inpatient to outpatient programs).

In principle, the "average" approach includes in the financial calculations the extent of so-called fixed expenditures associated with operating a particular program. Fixed expenditures in a hospital setting would include costs of heating, lighting, building maintenance, administration, recordkeeping, and so on, which are relatively independent of the actual number of inpatients. The "marginal" approach, on the other hand, chiefly emphasizes the "variable" costs of program operation. In the hospital environment variable costs are mainly the salaries and fringe benefits of direct care staff whose numbers might vary with the inpatient census. Because the "average" approach typically includes both fixed and variable costs in its financial impact calculations, the resulting figures may be larger than those obtained from the "marginal" approach. However, in some cases (e.g., having to hire expensive temporary staff to deal with a sudden hospital census increase), the marginal costs may be greater than the average.

Typically, the "average" approach will be more appropriate in situations where the fixed costs will change substantially. An example would be the case of hospital closure. Conversely, adding a relatively small number of patients to an existing program would best be handled by the "marginal" approach. Abolishing the outpatient component of the PSRB would be an intermediate case. If the PSRB's outpatient program is discontinued, Oregon would be obliged to open additional forensic wards but need not create an entirely new hospital.

REFERENCES

1. LaFond JQ, Durham ML: Back to Asylum: The Future of Mental Health Law and Policy in the United States. New York, Oxford University Press, 1992
2. Cutler DL, Bigelow DA, McFarland BH: The cost of fragmented mental health financing: is it worth it? Community Ment Health J 28:121–133, 1992
3. Bigelow DA, Bloom JD, Williams MH: Costs of managing insanity acquittees under a Psychiatric Security Review Board system. Hosp Community Psychiatry 41:613–621, 1990
4. Rubin J: Economic aspects of law and psychiatry. Int J Law Psychiatry 14:299–304, 1991
5. McFarland BH, Faulkner LR, Bloom JD, et al: Family members' opinions about civil commitment. Hosp Community Psychiatry 41:537–541, 1990
6. Lippincott RC: Developing mental health services in Oregon 1990–1995: Document III (Progress Report and Five-Year Blueprint for System Development). Salem, OR, Mental Health and Developmental Disabilities Services Division, 1990
7. Mental Health and Developmental Disabilities Services Division: 1991–1993 Mental Health Service Element Rates With Cost of Living—as of Nov. 13, 1991. Salem, OR, Mental Health and Developmental Disabilities Services Division, 1991
8. Lippincott RC: Developing mental health services in Oregon 1989–1995: Document II (Incorporating Progress as of September 30, 1989). Salem, OR, Mental Health and Developmental Disabilities Services Division, 1989
9. McFarland BH, Faulkner LR, Bloom JD, et al: Chronic mental illness and the criminal justice system. Hosp Community Psychiatry 40:718–724, 1989
10. Wyatt RJ: Neuroleptics and the natural course of schizophrenia. Schizophr Bull 17:325–351, 1991

11. Udvarhelyi IS, Colditz GA, Rai A, et al: Cost-effectiveness and cost-benefit analysis in the medical literature: are the methods being used correctly? Ann Intern Med 116:238–244, 1992

12. Guyatt GH, Jaeschke R: Measurements in clinical trials: choosing the appropriate approach, in Quality of Life Assessments in Clinical Trials. Edited by Spilker B. New York, Raven, 1990, pp 37–46

13. Samuelson PA, Nordhaus WD: Economics, 14th Edition. New York, McGraw-Hill, 1992

Chapter 12

Conditional Release as a National Standard for the Treatment of Insanity Acquittees

On a single day in 1986, there were 5,424 institutionalized insanity acquittees in the United States, with 271 hospitalized in Oregon. Oregon ranked third behind the District of Columbia and Hawaii in per capita hospitalization of insanity acquittees, with a rate of 10.04 per 100,000 compared with a national average of 2.25 per 100,000 (1). Looking at these figures from another perspective, Oregon had 5% of the nation's insanity acquittees in its hospital system, with 99% hospitalized in the state forensic unit and 1% with civil patients on other state hospital inpatient units. At the same time in 1986 in Oregon, there were approximately 120 insanity acquittees on conditional release in the community.

Given the relatively large numbers of insanity acquittees in Oregon, this book has described a system that from one point of view could be considered anomalous. Oregon, with a comparatively small population, has jurisdiction over an appreciable percentage of the nation's insanity acquittees.

The fact that the Oregon situation is anomalous with regard to the large number of insanity acquittees under its jurisdiction may have encouraged the pioneering of a large-scale conditional release program. In this area there clearly are lessons to be learned that can be applied to the treatment of insanity acquittees and other mentally ill offenders in other jurisdictions.

When we first read the statutes creating the Psychiatric Security Review Board (PSRB) (2) and began studying the system (3, 4), we believed that it had unique features. This potential was

first recognized on the national level following the Hinckley verdict, when there was a great deal of controversy about the insanity defense and the procedures designed for managing insanity
acquittees. The position statement on the insanity defense published by the American Psychiatric Association in 1983 (5) identified the PSRB as a promising model. In 1985, Connecticut became
the second state to implement a PSRB (6), and in 1989 Utah
passed similar legislation. Interest in this system remains high,
with other states actively considering Review Board or analogous
models (7).

In 1991, we published an article in the *American Journal of
Psychiatry* that focused on the monitored conditional release of
insanity acquittees (8). This report highlighted conditional release and monitored community treatment as a unique feature of
the Oregon system. Since the publication of that article in 1991
and the completion of this book in 1993, further developments in
this field have reinforced our belief that there is no longer any
reason for state forensic programs to be overwhelmingly inpatient oriented. We have chosen to focus on this subject in this
concluding chapter. We will build and expand on the major
conclusion of our 1991 article: *that the development of a conditional
release program should be a requirement for all state forensic programs
charged with the responsibility of caring for insanity acquittees.*

LEGAL ISSUES AND THE QUESTION OF FAIRNESS IN THE TREATMENT OF MENTALLY ILL OFFENDERS

As we discussed in relation to misdemeanants in Chapter 9, there
are critical concerns about stigmatization and fairness in relation
to societal treatment of mentally ill people (9). Concerns about
stigma are even more acute for those mentally ill individuals who
are also criminal offenders. This is true because of the frequently
perceived association of mental illness and dangerousness. This
question of heightened stigma for the mentally ill offender was
graphically illustrated in *United States ex rel. Schuster v. Herold*
(10), a 1969 case that concerned the transfer of a New York State
prisoner to a mental hospital. The court determined that such

transfers demanded procedural safeguards similar to those provided in civil commitment hearings and recognized these individuals as "twice cursed" with the stigma associated both with mental illness and criminality. This decision followed the reasoning set out in *Baxstrom v. Herold* (11), the U.S. Supreme Court's 1966 decision that required the use of civil commitment procedures in order to retain mentally ill offenders in mental hospitals after the expiration of their criminal sentences.

These cases were decided in an era of legal change that greatly enhanced the rights of mentally ill individuals in relation to civil commitment (12–15). The courts extended these key reforms to those found incompetent to stand trial (16); to insanity acquittees (17); to convicted sex offenders (18); and to those, as illustrated by *Baxstrom* and *Schuster*, who were in prison.

From the legal point of view, the attempt to obtain fair treatment for mentally ill people in the 1960s and 1970s resulted in the development of consistent legal procedures that were to be applied to mentally ill individuals across various categories of involuntary institutionalization. It was clear in *Baxstrom*, however, that the Supreme Court would not require identical procedures for all hearings involving mentally ill people. Variation in procedures based on the legal status of the mentally ill person persists to this day. This principle forms the basis of the ability of the Oregon PSRB to treat a mentally ill insanity acquittee differently from one who was civilly committed. What thus emerge from the era of legal change are procedural protections that are stringent but not identical for the various categories of mentally ill individuals.

Controversy continues about the viability of the insanity defense and its place in the criminal justice and mental health systems. There are those with strongly held views advocating for the elimination of the insanity defense (19), and others who view this defense as critical to the moral underpinnings of criminal law (20). This public opinion waxes and wanes along with the media coverage of the latest sensationalized insanity trial. Assuming that the insanity defense remains intact and the courts continue to find individuals not guilty by reason of insanity, questions arise as to how these individuals are to be managed by forensic mental health systems. Keilitz and Fulton (21) looked for a middle ground between civil commitment standards and the possibility of indefinite commitment found acceptable to the Supreme Court in *Jones v. United States* (22). In general, they favored the approach of the American Bar Association (23), which recommended separate commitment procedures for those who are acquitted by reason of insanity of dangerous felonies, reserving civil commitment procedures for misdemeanors and nondangerous felonies.

The legal approach to fairness has thus focused heavily on procedural protection. This is very important, but it is our view that models designed to achieve fairness for insanity acquittees must go beyond procedural protection and must include a focus on the treatment program provided to these mentally ill individuals. Our argument is that a key element in the overall treatment program is the availability of conditional release and monitored community treatment, which we consider the major advances in procedures related to the management of insanity acquittees during the 1980s.

MONITORED CONDITIONAL RELEASE

Most state forensic systems are heavily focused on inpatient services. Based on the evidence presented in this book, we think that such systems are simply inadequate to meet the legitimate liberty interests of a large number of insanity acquittees who could be conditionally released from the hospital and treated safely in monitored community treatment programs.

The release of insanity acquittees from forensic hospitals presents the decisionmaker with the traditional task of balancing protection of society with the liberty interests of insanity acquittees. In the last decade of this century, it seems clear that the protection of society has assumed dominance over these individuals' liberty interests. The way to maximize societal protection is to institutionalize many if not most insanity acquittees for as long as possible. With the advent of conditional release programs, and with their demonstrated effectiveness, this approach should no longer be considered acceptable.

Conditional release, monitored community treatment, and the

availability of workable revocation procedures provide practical means of addressing the issue of balanced dispositions for insanity acquittees. Three areas are critical when we discuss the benefits of a conditional release program. These areas are the prediction of dangerousness, the provision of psychiatric care, and the costs of conditional release.

The Prediction of Dangerousness

Any system designed to deal with mentally ill forensic patients must address the complicated problem of societal protection as embodied in the question of the prediction of dangerousness. Once an individual has raised a successful insanity defense, the prediction of dangerousness becomes a key problem for the decisionmaker. In fact, there is no other single issue that has raised more concern in the legal and psychiatric communities than the accuracy of the prediction of future dangerousness (24). The currently accepted position in the scientific community is that the long-term prediction of dangerousness cannot be made with any acceptable degree of accuracy (25–27). Yet this is exactly the determination that is called for on a regular basis when a judge, or a body such as the PSRB, must decide whether to hospitalize, conditionally release, or discharge an insanity acquittee.

Effective mechanisms for conditional release and revocation make the issue of predicting dangerous behavior less pressing, because the system takes up the slack for the potential inaccuracy of the prediction. Society in general and the legal community in particular tend to view dangerousness as a trait that an individual possesses, rendering the person either dangerous or not dangerous. Psychiatry and the behavioral sciences, on the other hand, view dangerousness more as a state that is greatly influenced by changes in the person's mental status and support network. In this model, if the individual is on conditional release and if mental status and social situation are monitored, there is a great likelihood that negative changes will be apparent early and that this will allow time for corrective action.

A treatment system that has limited community options will inevitably be pressured into placing greater weight on the prediction of dangerousness because of the significant negative consequences of a release error. Such systems will hospitalize individuals for longer periods of time than would be necessary if the proper community system was in place. Monitored community treatment provides a method to address the issue of the protection of society while simultaneously serving the legitimate liberty interests of insanity acquittees by developing treatment in the least restrictive setting.

Chapter 4 focused on the hospitalization and conditional release of subjects in this study. In that chapter, we presented data regarding criminal recidivism of subjects on conditional release. There were 41 felony and 43 misdemeanor crimes charged against 15% of the conditionally released subjects in 8,321 months of conditional release. As we said in that chapter, we leave it to the reader to put his or her own value judgment to these figures. Clearly, conditionally released subjects in Oregon are charged with relatively few crimes, both on an absolute basis and when compared with their behavior before and after PSRB jurisdiction.

Revocation is a critical part of this equation. Fifty percent of conditionally released subjects were revoked at some point during their conditional release and returned to the forensic hospital. Wiederanders's recent report from California (28) presents even more favorable data than we have presented in this book. Although these findings need to be qualified by the length of the follow-up period, the report presents findings that are similar to what we report. The recent study from Maryland (29) presents data indicating a higher frequency of arrests for conditionally released subjects. The authors report plans for the development of more intensive monitoring for their outpatients. Although it was not addressed in the article, we believe that the intensity of the supervision and the availability of procedures for prompt revocation are the key factors in reducing police contacts of conditionally released insanity acquittees. These are the features that reduce the pressures on the institutional psychiatrist and on the decisionmaker to predict dangerousness.

**Psychiatric Issues—The Treatment System
and the Insanity Acquittee**

The provision of adequate psychiatric treatment for insanity acquittees depends primarily on the nature and intensity of their mental illnesses and whether effective treatment programs exist that can address these illnesses and the needs of these individuals for social support.

The insanity defense is designed to remove seriously mentally ill individuals from the criminal justice system. The defense demands that insanity acquittees have significant deficiencies of reason that set them apart from other offenders charged with similar crimes. However, concepts of legal insanity and psychiatric insanity can become confused, with the result that legal tests for insanity may produce a group of individuals that psychiatrists currently do not know how to treat effectively.

The potential harm created by the confusion between definitions can be illustrated by an example outside of the insanity defense per se, in Oregon's dangerous offender statute. The dangerous offender statute allows Oregon judges to lengthen the sentence of certain criminal offenders based on the report of a psychiatrist or a psychologist that the individual "suffered from a severe personality disorder with a propensity for violent crime" (30). This statute, in effect, created a group of dangerous offenders in Oregon's prisons, each of whom psychiatrists or psychologists diagnosed as having a "severe personality disorder" with violent propensities—in a sense, a legally based type of mental illness. This was the situation until recently, when a group of inmates, with this legally determined form of mental illness sued the state, claiming that their diagnosed mental illnesses were not being treated. A trial court judge found in their favor. The state was then faced with the problem of having to provide treatment for a group of inmates whom most of the mental health community did not consider mentally ill, and for whom there were no viable treatment techniques available.

In this situation the statute created a type of legal "insanity." Unfortunately, some psychiatrists and psychologists testified as to its existence, and the courts found that those with this condition were entitled to treatment. The state was then required to treat a condition that most of the mental health community considered not treatable. The point is that legal and psychiatric insanity do not necessarily define the same phenomena and, further, that there may be no psychiatric treatment for some legally defined mental illness.

There are similar concerns here for the insanity defense and how it is used in relation to the group of individuals it defines as insanity acquittees. Issues debated in the past focused on the interpretation of insanity tests. For example, during the era of psychoanalytic theory's preeminence in psychiatric thought, there were attempts to reconcile the theories of the unconscious with the *Durham* or product test for insanity (31). Current discussions emphasize problems created by societal pressure to make dangerousness, in and of itself, a form of mental illness and thereby transform hospitals into detention centers for some dangerous offenders who are not mentally ill (32, 33). Given the dangers of confusing legal and psychiatric insanity, does the insanity defense produce a group of acquittees who can be treated by psychiatrists and other mental health professionals? The answer from our data is predominantly yes, with some reservations. In Chapter 3, we reported on the characteristics of subjects in this study. The typical insanity acquittee in Oregon is an unmarried, unemployed white male in his early 30s who has schizophrenia and who had a history at the time that Oregon judges committed him to the jurisdiction of the PSRB of 3.1 prior psychiatric hospitalizations and 4.05 contacts with the criminal justice system. This prototypical individual is chronically mentally ill; and although this is not clearly supported by our data, he has a high likelihood of also having a substance abuse disorder.

Chapter 8 focused on psychiatric diagnosis. In addition to an emphasis on the major mental illnesses of schizophrenia and bipolar disorder, this chapter pointed out some of the problems related to acquittees with personality disorders and mental retardation. These subject groups accounted for slightly under 20% of the sample. Although they are a relatively small subset, they pose many challenges to the system, and their needs and their resulting impact on the system should not be minimized. However, the vast majority of the acquittees in this sample are chronically mental ill and have treatable mental illnesses.

Both schizophrenia and mania are diseases for which extensive progress has been made in biological treatment of these disorders. In addition, in the 1980s major advances were made in the psychosocial treatments for these disorders, with the development of focused community treatment programs for chronically mentally ill people. Community programs based on the principles of psychosocial rehabilitation are critical to the treatment of chronically mentally ill patients (34–36), and the treatment approach for such patients is applicable to chronically mentally ill insanity acquittee. The conditional release of insanity acquittees provides the opportunity to apply these developing community treatment technologies to the treatment of these individuals.

Chapter 6 detailed the treatment provided to insanity acquittees in this sample. The treatment described in this chapter is consistent with community support models, with heavy reliance on case management, psychiatric evaluation, medication management, and various other supportive services including sheltered housing.

These models clearly fit the needs of many chronically mentally ill individuals. We have written elsewhere (37) about the need for a greater accommodation between legal and psychiatric concepts of insanity so as to have a truly functional insanity defense. We believe that to a large extent this is happening with regard to Oregon's insanity acquittees.

Costs of Providing Conditional Release Services

Costs were addressed in Chapter 11. This is an area that deserves further work as part of a mental health services research agenda. Our earlier paper (38) reported that a conditional release mechanism reduced costs of the forensic system when compared with a hypothetical model that was much more heavily inpatient oriented. This was also reported in the Wiederanders article (28) from California, which indicated that the cost of maintaining an acquittee on conditional release was estimated to be one-fifth the cost of having the same person in a forensic hospital. With favorable data on public safety and on treatment models, this area cannot be ignored.

CONCLUSION

Over the past 25 years, during which major changes took place in the laws relating to mentally ill offenders, there were also major developments in the field of psychiatry. Great enthusiasm accompanied both the advent of an expanded number of medications for mentally ill people and changes in the delivery of mental health services brought about by the community mental health center movement (39). Much was accomplished during this period in both psychiatry and the law to improve the lives of mentally ill citizens. Few will lament the changes brought about in traditional state hospitals, and many mentally ill individuals have made successful adjustments in the community. However, the wave of legal reforms and the rapid changes that accompanied the community mental health center movement also fueled the negative consequences of deinstitutionalization. The casualties of unplanned deinstitutionalization are now apparent everywhere. This is evident in the mounting number of homeless mentally ill people (40, 41) and in "transinstitutionalization" (42) that has led so many people with mental illness to nursing homes or (as we have seen here) to the criminal justice system. It is a sad characterization of our times that it is anecdotally reported that the Los Angeles County Jail is the largest mental hospital in southern California.

The conclusion of this chapter and a major conclusion of this book is that the development of conditional release—monitored community treatment with the possibility of prompt revocation—provides a mechanism to achieve a fair and balanced treatment experience for insanity acquittees. This helps society provide the acquittee with a reasonable treatment program that conforms to standards set for other mentally ill individuals. In psychiatry today, a treatment system that is solely or even predominately institutionally based should be judged inadequate. Programs for patients with severe mental illnesses, analogous to those available to the typical insanity acquittee, are designed along a continuum ranging from inpatient to outpatient treatment. As we have pointed out, programs designed for chronically mentally ill people—such as activity and socialization groups, day treatment, sheltered living and work, and dual diagnosis treatment modules—fit well into this continuum. Monitored community treatment is another aspect of this approach tailored to the needs of a segment of this population involved with the criminal justice system. This approach also has important implications for civil commitment (43).

We have relied for too long on simplistic models for hospitalization and community care. A patient was either in or out of the hospital; there was no middle ground. A realistic appraisal of the needs of chronically mentally ill people as described in this book cries out for a different model. Episodic care does not work. We need a longer-term perspective for the treatment of these patients. We also need to provide for such care both in hospitals and in the community—with the caveat that the community care should be designed realistically, with conditions set forth that will foster positive adjustment.

The data presented in this book support these conclusions. However, data from one state—especially one that we have acknowledged is anomalous among jurisdictions in how it uses the insanity defense—are not adequate to support the development of program standards that would apply across this country. There has been increasing interest in the area of conditional release over the past decade. In addition to our work in Oregon (44, 45), there are data from Maryland (46–48), Illinois (49, 50), California (28, 51–53), New York (54), and Washington, DC (55), all of which support this position. In addition to a developing empirical base, there are recent articles that propose guidelines for those interested in developing monitored outpatient treatment programs (56–58).

All of these reports highlight the effectiveness of conditional release and monitored community support treatment programs for the management and treatment of insanity acquittees. We have a model in which law, psychiatry, and the related mental health fields can work together, relatively harmoniously, toward common goals. Our conclusion is that there is now enough information known about insanity acquittees, and about the principles underlying conditional release programs, to require that forensic programs in all jurisdictions adopt such programs. Such a requirement would move us substantially in the direction of what Wexler and Winick have called for, namely the development of programs dedicated to the principles of "therapeutic jurisprudence" (59).

REFERENCES

1. Way BB, Dvoskin JA, Steadman HJ: Forensic psychiatric inpatients served in the United States: regional and system differences. Bull Am Acad Psychiatry Law 19:405–412, 1991
2. Bloom JD, Bloom JL: Disposition of insanity defense cases in Oregon. Bull Am Acad Psychiatry Law 9, 1981
3. Rogers JL, Bloom JD, Manson SM: Oregon's reform of the insanity defense system. Hosp Community Psychiatry 33:1022–1023, 1982
4. Rogers JL, Bloom JD: Characteristics of persons committed to Oregon's Psychiatric Security Review Board. Bull Am Acad Psychiatry Law 10:155–165, 1982
5. Insanity Defense Work Group: American Psychiatric Association statement on the insanity defense. Am J Psychiatry 140:681–688, 1983
6. Scott D, Zonana H, Gatz M: Monitoring insanity acquittees: Connecticut's Psychiatric Security Review Board. Hosp Community Psychiatry 41:980–984, 1990
7. McGreevy MA, Steadman HJ, Dvoskin JA, et al: New York State's system of managing insanity acquittees in the community. Hosp Community Psychiatry 42:512–517, 1991
8. Bloom JD, Williams MH, Bigelow DA: Monitored conditional release of persons found not guilty by reason of insanity. Am J Psychiatry 148:444–448, 1991
9. Fink PJ, Tasman A (eds): Stigma and Mental Illness. Washington, DC, American Psychiatric Press, 1992
10. United States ex rel. Schuster v Herold, 410 F.2d 1071, cert den 396 US 847 (2d Cir. 1969)
11. Baxstrom v Herold, 383 US 107, 86 S. Ct. 760, 15 L.Ed.2d 620 (1966)
12. Stone AA: Mental Health and Law: A System in Transition (DHEW Publ No ADM-76-176). Washington, DC, U.S. Government Printing Office, 1975
13. Wyatt v Stickney, 344 F.Supp 387 (MD Ala. 1972)
14. O'Connor v Donaldson, 442 US 563 (1975)
15. Miller RD: Involuntary Civil Commitment of the Mentally Ill in the Post-Reform Era. Springfield, IL, Charles C Thomas, 1987
16. Jackson v Indiana, 406 US 715, 192 S. Ct. 1845, 32 L.Ed.2d 435 (1972)

17. Bolton v Harris, 395 F.2d 642 (D.C. Cir. 1968)
18. Specht v Patterson, 386 US 605, 87 S. Ct. 1209, 18 L.Ed.d 326 (1967)
19. Morris N: Madness and the Criminal Law. Chicago, IL, University of Chicago Press, 1982
20. Bonnie RJ: The moral basis of the insanity defense. American Bar Association Journal 69:194–197, 1983
21. Keilitz I, Fulton JP: The Insanity Defense and Its Alternatives. Washington, DC, National Center for State Courts, 1984, R-085
22. Jones v United States, 463 US 354, 103 S. Ct. 3043, 77 L.Ed.2d 694 (1983)
23. Standard 7-6.1. The Defense of Insanity: American Bar Association Standing Committee on Association Standards for Criminal Justice. Washington, DC, American Bar Association, 1983, pp 260–273
24. Cocozza J, Steadman HJ: The failure of psychiatric predictions of dangerousness: clear and convincing evidence. Rutgers Law Review 29:1074–1101, 1976
25. Monahan J: The Clinical Prediction of Violent Behavior (DHHS Publ No ADM-81-921). Rockville, MD, National Institute of Mental Health, 1981
26. Monahan J: The prediction of violent behavior: toward a second generation of theory and policy. Am J Psychiatry 141:10–15, 1984
27. Shah SA: Dangerousness: conceptual prediction and public policy issues, in Violence and Violent Individuals. Edited by Hay JR, Roberts TK, Solway KS. New York, SP Medical & Scientific Books, 1981, pp 151–177
28. Wiederanders MR: Recidivism of disordered offenders who were conditionally vs. unconditionally released. Behavioral Sciences and the Law 10:141–148, 1992
29. Tellefsen C, Cohen MI, Silver SB, et al: Predicting success on conditional release for insanity acquittees: regionalized versus nonregionalized hospital patients. Bull Am Acad Psychiatry Law 20:87–100, 1992
30. Oregon Revised Statutes §161.725
31. Blocker v United States, 288 F.2d 853 (D.C. Cir. 1961)
32. Appelbaum PS: The new preventive detention: psychiatry's problematic responsibility for the control of violence. Am J Psychiatry 145:779–785, 1988
33. Foucha v Louisiana, 563 So.2d 1138 (La. 1990); 112 S. Ct. 1780, 1992
34. Lamb HR: Treating the Long-Term Mentally Ill: Beyond Deinstitutionalization. San Francisco, CA, Jossey-Bass, 1983

35. Talbott JA: The Chronic Mental Patient—Five Years Later. New York, Grune & Stratton, 1984

36. Solomon P, Davis J, Gordon B: Discharged state hospital patients' characteristics and use of aftercare: effect on community tenure. Am J Psychiatry 141:1566–1570, 1984

37. Bloom JD, Bradford J, Kofed L: An overview of treatment approaches to three offender groups. Hosp Community Psychiatry 39:151–158, 1988

38. Bigelow DA, Bloom JD, Williams MH: Costs of managing insanity acquittees under a psychiatric security review board system. Hosp Community Psychiatry 41:613–614, 1990

39. Foley HA, Sharfstein SS: Madness and Government: Who Cares for the Mentally Ill. Washington, DC, American Psychiatric Press, 1983

40. Lamb HR (ed): The Homeless Mentally Ill: A Task Force Report of the American Psychiatric Association. Washington, DC, American Psychiatric Association, 1984

41. U.S. Department of Health and Human Services: Outcasts on Main Street: Report of the Federal Task Force on Homelessness and Severe Mental Illness (DHHS Publ No ADM-92-1904). Washington, DC, U.S. Government Printing Office, 1992

42. Talbott JA: Deinstitutionalization: avoiding the disasters of the past. Hosp Community Psychiatry 30:621–624, 1979

43. Geller JL: Clinical guidelines for the use of involuntary outpatient treatment. Hosp Community Psychiatry 41:749–755, 1990

44. Bloom JD, Rogers JL, Manson SM: After Oregon's insanity defense: a comparison of conditional release and hospitalization. Int J Law Psychiatry 5:391–402, 1982

45. Bloom JD, Williams MH, Rogers JL, et al: Evaluation and treatment of insanity acquittees in the community. Bull Am Acad Psychiatry Law 14:231–244, 1986

46. Goldmeier J, White EV, Ulrich C, et al: Community intervention with the mentally ill offender: a residential program. Bull Am Acad Psychiatry Law 8:72–81, 1980

47. Spodak MK, Silver SB, Wright CU: Criminality of discharged insanity acquittees: fifteen year experience in Maryland reviewed. Bull Am Acad Psychiatry Law 12:373–382, 1984

48. Silver SB, Tellefsen C: Administrative issues in the follow-up treatment of insanity acquittees. Journal of Mental Health Administration 18:242–252, 1991

49. Rogers R, Cavanaugh JL: A program for potentially violent offender patients. International Journal of Offender Therapy and Comparative Criminology 25:53–59, 1981

50. Cavanaugh JL, Wasyliw OE: Adjustment of the not guilty by reason of insanity (NGRI) outpatient: an initial report. J Forensic Sci 30:24–30, 1985

51. Lamb HR, Weinberger LE, Gross BH: Court-mandated community outpatient treatment for persons found Not Guilty by Reason of Insanity: a five-year follow-up. Am J Psychiatry 145:450–456, 1988

52. Lamb HR, Weinberger LE, Gross BH: Court-mandated outpatient treatment for insanity acquittees: clinical philosophy and implementation. Hosp Community Psychiatry 39:1080–1084, 1988

53. Wiederanders M: The effectiveness of the conditional release program. Sacramento, CA, California Department of Mental Health, 1990

54. Callahan L: Comparing programs for monitoring NGRIs. NIMH Research Proposal (R29 MH44258-01A1). Delmar, NY, Policy Research Associates, 1990

55. National Institute of Mental Health: Ad Hoc Forensic Advisory Panel: Final Report. Washington, DC, National Institute of Mental Health, September 1987

56. Meloy JR, Haroun A, Schiller EF: Clinical Guidelines for Involuntary Outpatient Treatment. Sarasota, FL, Professional Resource Exchange Inc, 1990

57. Griffin PA, Steadman HJ, Heilbrun K: Designing conditional release systems for insanity acquittees. Journal of Mental Health Administration 18:231–241, 1991

58. Wexler DB: Health care compliance principles and the insanity acquittees conditional release process. Criminal Law Bulletin 27:18–41, 1991

59. Wexler DB, Winick BJ: Essays in Therapeutic Jurisprudence. Durham, NC, Carolina Academic Press, 1991

Index

*Page numbers printed in **boldface** type refer to tables or figures.*